NOTES ON THE
CARE & CATALOGUING
OF OLD MAPS

KENNIKAT PRESS SCHOLARLY REPRINTS

Dr. Ralph Adams Brown, Senior Editor

Series on
MAN AND HIS ENVIRONMENT
Under the General Editorial Supervision of
Dr. Roger C. Heppell
Professor of Geography, State University of New York

NOTES ON THE
CARE & CATALOGUING
OF OLD MAPS

BY LLOYD A. BROWN

KENNIKAT PRESS
Port Washington, N. Y./London

NOTES ON THE CARE & CATALOGUING OF OLD MAPS

First published in 1941
Reissued in 1970 by Kennikat Press
Library of Congress Catalog Card No: 76-113281
ISBN 0-8046-1319-2

Manufactured by Taylor Publishing Company   Dallas, Texas

KENNIKAT SERIES ON MAN AND HIS ENVIRONMENT

To

My Friend

F. E. DRAGOO

CONTENTS

INTRODUCTION

While manuscripts have been collected for more
than four thousand years, the making of maps and the
dissemination of geographic information was restricted
for centuries by political and religious forces and by
the mysterious and secret nature of the information
associated with maps and charts. At the beginning of
the Christian era only the brave and the pagan in-
dulged in geographic speculation. It was a sin to probe
the mysteries of the universe, and the explanations
set forth by the church in regard to the heavens and
the earth were sufficiently vague and awe-inspiring
to satisfy all but the most skeptical observers of natural phenomena. So, while manuscripts were collected
openly, maps were made furtively, studied secretly and
in many cases destroyed promptly.

Maps have long been associated with military intel-
ligence as well as with adventure and intrigue. Because they were potential sources of information to the
enemy, it was dangerous to plot on maps and charts
the location of roads and navigable streams by which
an army might approach a city. It was equally dangerous to inform the hostile world of the location of military objectives such as arsenals, barracks, dockyards,
banks and public buildings. Therefore many rulers

were afraid to make good maps and charts, and were even more loathe to collect and preserve them. J. G. Kohl[1] relates that the Roman emperor Augustus locked up the maps resulting from his extensive survey of the realm, and issued only partial copies to the imperial councilors of his provinces. As late as the nineteenth century it was considered an act of high treason to divulge the information on official maps, and it is safe to say that today every government agency, both here and abroad, has maps of a confidential nature which are guarded as carefully as international boundaries themselves. Sea charts, too, have been jealously guarded for ages, especially those made after the discovery of the New World. Maritime trade routes, avenues of wealth as well as "life-lines," were and still are vital to certain nations, and charts which plotted the courses of merchant fleets across the seas were very important documents. Early navigators, especially the enterprising Spanish and Portuguese explorers of the sixteenth century, made a practice of weighting their charts with lead; and when their ships were boarded by the enemy, they threw the charts overboard rather than let the foe profit by their hard-earned information about the high seas. Such customs were not favorable to the general dissemination of geographic information, nor did they contribute to a wide appreciation of the value and importance of maps and charts.

Map production received its first real impetus in the fifteenth century. Within the short space of 50 years the printing press was invented and developed, Ptolemy's *Geographia* was revived and the New World

----

[1] Kohl, J. G. Substance of a lecture . . . on . . . maps of America. (In Smithsonian institution. Annual report, 1856.) Washington, 1857, p. 93–146.

was discovered. But at this very time, when maps were being published in rapidly increasing quantities to meet the changing ideas of the configuration of the earth, and to keep up with the "new discoveries" in the Western Hemisphere, a new trend appeared which delayed for many years the systematic collecting and preserving of cartographic material. This was the tendency to discard old maps for new.

It is not strange that people should assume that the latest will naturally be the best, whether it be automobiles or maps; but it is unreasonable to assume, in the case of maps, that because a map is out of date it is of no value and consequently should not be allowed to take up space. The best maps and charts are nearly always compilations of data taken from other reliable maps and charts. Keeping this fact in mind, let us suppose it possible to produce a perfect map, embodying all the information which could be gleaned from previously compiled sources. Would there be any excuse for discarding and destroying the sources from which it was compiled? If there were, the same reasoning applied to books and manuscripts would eliminate most libraries and all archival collections. And yet there is evidence which indicates that this destructive tendency has operated continuously for hundreds of years and still persists to a certain extent.

Maps did not come into their own, did not "attain the dignity of historical documents," according to Kohl, until the beginning of the nineteenth century, when a few farsighted European scholars began to search musty archives and dark corners of book stalls for the long lost keystones of historical cartography. They found some of them, but many were apparently gone forever. Baron Charles Athanese Walckenaer (1771–1852) is usually given the credit for arousing interest in the subject of early cartography because of his writings and the exploitation of the remarkable collection of source material which he assembled in his Paris home. Edme Jomard contributed much towards the formation of a branch of the Imperial Library in Paris, in which were gathered remarkable examples of ancient cartography which had been forgotten and "lost" for many years. The Polish scholar Joachim Lelewel and the Portuguese Vicomte de Santarem stimulated the interest and appreciation of other scholars by publishing facsimiles of important maps and charts, accompanied by learned dissertations.

The vigorous efforts of a few scholars, supported by a generally awakened interest in antiquities, resulted in the formation of many great collections in the latter part of the nineteenth century, and others have since been formed. Today it is constantly reasserted that the civilized world is becoming more and more "map conscious." But in spite of the alleged status of maps at the present time, there has been a decided lag between the growth of interest in the subject and the development of administrative technique. This situation is due, in a large measure, to the traditional attitude of considering maps as minor publications and administering them as such. As reference tools, maps are seldom given major consideration. As minor publications maps are catalogued and classified after all other material has been taken care of, which means that they seldom receive the attention they deserve. Maps cannot be properly administered as adjuncts to the newspaper or periodical collection of a library.

Taking into account these various inhibitory factors, it is not strange that there is a lack of well-established rules and procedures governing the administration of maps and charts, nor is it surprising that card catalogues and systems of classification are not considered essential aids to the use of map collections.

It has been said that the cataloguing of maps and related material does not require a special set of rules, that maps may be catalogued according to the rules established for the cataloguing of printed books. Those who have tried to apply these rules to old maps, however, are inclined to question this assertion. There are numerous irregularities of form and content among old maps which have not been adequately covered by existing rules of cataloguing. Yet in spite of the fact that there are no firmly established rules to guide the cataloguer, it is possible, even essential, to make some sort of a card catalogue an integral part of every map collection. Even a skeleton catalogue is better than none, and an author or title entry and a single subject card for every map, whether that map be in sheet form or in a book, will soon prove its worth to the librarian and the reader. There is enough information on every printed map to warrant its transposition to ·a card, and very few manuscript maps have so little on them that it is impossible to identify the area delineated, or to designate the general significance of the map, even though the cartographer and the date are unknown.

Several essays and guides on the subject of map administration have been published over a period of years. They represent the study and experience of trained individuals who have worked with large map collections wherein some sort of plan was absolutely essential to the efficient economy of the material. Each of these works was based primarily on methods which had proved best for the management of one particular map collection. Therefore, the possibility of adapting any one of these systems to map collections other than that for which it was specifically designed was naturally of secondary consideration.

A comparative study of the various systems employed in cataloguing and classifying maps yields interesting results. All have two purposes in common. First, they are designed to make it possible to locate material in the collection with ease and with a minimum loss of time. Second, each system is designed to bring together in the map file all closely related material. The former purpose is of course the essence of all library economy; the latter is the aim of all systems of library classification. It is noticeable, furthermore, that most of the important differences in the systems of map classification in print and in operation resolve themselves into the interpretation of the phrase "related material" and the methods of classifying and filing that material.

The observations on map administration in the following pages are also based on the experience of the writer with a specific collection of maps, a highly specialized collection containing nothing but *old* maps, charts, plans and geographic atlases, and one in which material relating to American history is strongly emphasized. However, in spite of the limited size and scope of the collection which forms the background of these observations, a good deal of thought has been given to the possible extension and application of rules and procedures to larger and more general collections.

The writer has spent a great deal of time analyzing the data which are treated in the cataloguing and classification of printed books in an effort to find corresponding data on maps which could and should receive similar treatment. Although the task seemed impossible at first, it was surprising to find how readily cartographic data, with a few conspicuous exceptions, fall into the technical pattern worked out for printed books. Since making this discovery, every effort has been made to effect a transposition of established rules and procedures. When analogous situations were lacking, the writer tried to find some established rule which could be applied in modified form to the new situation. At this point it should be said that the following pages are to be considered more as a guide to the making of rules than as a rule book. It is not expected that all solutions to cataloguing and classification problems outlined herein will meet the needs of every map collection or the approval of every cataloguer, though the general plan should work without difficulty.

The scope of this work is limited, for the sake of convenience, to those maps which were made and printed between 1500 and 1800. Many exceptions to every rule are thus avoided. However, these limiting dates do not necessarily preclude the possibility of applying the same cataloguing and classification principles to maps printed after 1800; in fact the writer has tried to point out the necessity of a broad interpretation of all rules governing map administration.

Believing it impossible to appraise and analyze old maps intelligently without some knowledge of the history of cartography, the writer has devoted more space to historical background than would ordinarily be indicated in a cataloguing manual. In supplying this background the writer has drawn freely from the appended bibliography. Many of the works consulted are rich in anecdotes and bibliographic minutiae, and all are recommended to those who wish to read further on the subject.

The list of references is by no means exhaustive. Included in the list are a few books which cover each phase of early cartography. Also included are guides to the handling, cataloguing and classification of printed matter of all kinds. The catalogues and check lists are extremely valuable aids to the inexperienced cataloguer who has trouble dating or otherwise identifying old maps. The purpose of this type of bibliography is to give the librarian an idea of the size and scope of the field of cartography, and the kind of help he may expect to get from the literature on the subject. The illustrations are reproductions from original maps in the William L. Clements Library; the catalogue cards are from the file in the Map Division.

Several persons have contributed much time and professional knowledge towards the compilation of these *Notes*. I wish to express my sincere thanks to F. E. Dragoo, Mrs. Clara Egli Le Gear, Mrs. Dorothy C. Lewis, Miss Margaret Mann, Miss Elizabeth B. Steere, Miss Margaret N. Webber, Randolph G. Adams, S. W. Boggs, W. L. G. Joerg and Lawrence Martin for valuable suggestions, frank criticism and hearty coöperation. I am also indebted to the Horace H. Rackham School of Graduate Studies for its support of this enterprise. At the same time I accept full responsibility for the accuracy of all statements, historical or otherwise, herein set forth, and for the practicability of all administrative procedures suggested for the care and cataloguing of old maps.

LLOYD ARNOLD BROWN

Ann Arbor, Michigan
August 24, 1940.

I.

STORAGE AND EQUIPMENT

The chief problem of map administration, apart from cataloguing and classification, is the matter of storage and equipment. It is a problem which arises from the wide differences in size and form of geographic material. There are globes and relief maps, important items which require special storage facilities. There are sheet maps, roll maps, folded maps and maps enclosed in cases. Last of all there are maps in atlases and books. But except for globes and relief maps, which usually constitute a small percentage of any map collection, separate maps, i.e., sheet maps, roll maps and folding maps, are the chief concern of the librarian.

STORING SHEET MAPS

It is generally agreed that all maps should be stored flat. Unless a roll map is being used as a permanent wall display, it should be taken off its roll and flattened. Folded maps and maps in slipcases or boxes, many of which were so published, should be unfolded and treated as sheet maps. Exceptions may be made when rare maps, purchased in the original publishers' slipcases or boxes, are to be preserved for only occasional reference. Maps which are to be used constantly and exposed to a great deal of handling will soon

17

show wear if they are frequently removed from their cases, unfolded, refolded and replaced in their containers. The life of a box or slipcase submitted to constant handling by readers and staff is usually short.

Old maps fall logically into three general sizes: large, medium and small. These sizes are regulated by the size of the sheets of paper on which they were printed. All paper was made by hand prior to the year 1800. The size of the sheets so made was limited by the convenience with which a frame of pulp could be handled by the papermakers. Long years of experience showed that one man could handle a frame loaded with wet pulp large enough to make a sheet of paper about 28 × 24 inches. Larger frames were too heavy and awkward for one man to handle. Of course these dimensions varied from time to time and from place to place, but those mentioned above represent the average limit, and most old maps were printed on sheets of about this size, or on multiple or fractional parts thereof. The high cost of copper, and the amount of time and expense involved in the process of engraving also tended to limit map sizes. But larger maps exist, and these were made by engraving on two or more plates, printing on the same number of sheets, and afterwards pasting the sheets together.

Nearly all of the largest maps were originally bound into atlases. The "sheet" was folded once, the short way, and a volume made up of sheets so folded is known as folio size. Small maps were made in a size which could be printed on a sheet of paper made by folding and cutting the folio sheet the short way, making a sheet one half the size of a folio. A book or atlas made up of leaves so folded is known as a quarto volume. Still smaller maps were made by printing on half of the quarto leaf, making a size known as octavo.

Actually there are very few single-sheet maps extant which are as large as the basic sizes mentioned above. It has been pointed out that nearly all maps were made up into books or atlases. In the process of binding, the binder's knife or "plow" was used to trim off the edges on three sides, often without discretion; for this reason one need not expect to find many maps approaching standard sizes, although once in a great while a sheet escaped the binder's guillotine.

These facts are brought out because they should be considered in the selection of map-filing equipment, the dimensions of which should be based on the size of map most commonly encountered. The latter size, based on the most common sheet map, allowing for considerable variation, requires a tray or drawer 40 inches along the front and not less than 24 inches from front to back. Standard map equipment in use at the present time is built to accommodate maps of about this size. Drawers or trays may vary in one dimension or another by a few inches, but essentially they are designed to take care of the medium-sized sheet map. The Clements Library has units, each one of which contains fifteen drawers measuring 36 × 36 inches, and fifteen drawers 48 inches along the front and 36 inches from front to back. The larger drawers are very useful in that they permit filing a number of oversize maps, many of them rare manuscripts, without folding or cutting; but drawers of this size would not be required for the usual collection of old maps. In fact it is generally more desirable to use only one size of drawers for the map file, except when dealing with very small maps (*see* Small Maps). The width of the drawers in the Clements Library (front to back) is greater than is necessary; 30 inches would be adequate, and 24 inches would be possible.

Variations in the length and breadth of drawers are justified when they are to be used for a collection of maps which will never be shifted to other drawers or fed into another collection. For example, if the library has a collection of large wall maps, the gift of some friend of the library, which is to be kept as a unit permanently, it would be logical to have special cases or drawers built to accommodate the collection, regardless of size. On the other hand, cases which must suffice to hold any maps the library may acquire must be selected with that function in mind.

DEPTH OF DRAWERS

Map drawers or trays should be as shallow as possible; two and one half inches should be the maximum depth. When a deeper drawer is used, the pulling and hauling necessary to extract a map from the bottom of the pile is inefficient and is always bad for the map, even though it is protected by a stout folder. Also, there is more economy of space, up to a certain point, in shallow drawers than in deep ones. Reinforced construction is required for those deeper than two and one half inches, since beyond that depth a drawer full of maps becomes very heavy, especially if the maps are in protecting folders.

Map-filing equipment should be selected with care. There are many different types on the market, manufactured by firms which specialize in the design and construction of library and office equipment. As might be expected, there is considerable variation in price and quality in the offerings of different manufacturers. There are many small differences of design or construction which are unimportant, but which are calculated to suit different tastes. Other factors, such as the size and depth of drawers and the durability of the equipment are more important. The ease with which a drawer can be operated should not be overlooked. An empty drawer may slide back and forth without sticking, but the same one loaded with maps may be difficult to operate.

VERTICAL FILES

There are differences of opinion among librarians as to the efficiency of large vertical files for the storage of *old* maps. Some feel that they are efficient and economical; others testify that the system is detrimental to both map and folder. Paper that is from one to three hundred years old should not be subjected to the pulling and hauling necessary to extricate it from a vertical file. Many old maps will not support their own weight, no matter how carefully they are hinged or otherwise supported at the top. Also, there is little economy of space, if, to protect each map in the vertical file, a heavy folder is used to enclose it. Maps stored in this way are extremely hard to handle because it often takes two people to take out or replace a large map from the back of a vertical file. Certain types of improved plan files have strong supporters among librarians, and filing boxes similar to the old-style letter files are used to good advantage in the Clements Library Map Room, but only for filing small maps (*see* discussion under Small Maps).

MAP FOLDERS

Any map folder is better than none. A folder serves two purposes: it protects the map from dust while in storage and from direct handling while being taken out of, or being replaced in, a drawer; it also serves as a surface on which to write or print data, such as author, place of publication and date. An ordinary sheet of heavy wrapping paper, which is as much protection as many libraries can afford, will serve as a map folder. A stiff folder, of tag stock for example, is a better protection against careless handling, is not so likely to tear, and of course will wear much longer than an ordinary wrapping-paper folder. Experience plus considerable experimentation has shown that a 150-pound tag stock (there are many good ones sold under numerous trade names) is about the best for the purpose. Heavier weights prove too brittle and are very awkward to handle. Lighter weights are prone to crack or collapse or both, with handling.

When selecting a tag-stock folder, it is well to have in mind the labeling of the folder. Tag stock is made of wood pulp and does not always take ink well. Sizing is used in its manufacture, but the amount varies widely in different grades of paper. The better qualities have smooth, shiny surfaces. Such paper takes ink well and does not bruise easily, while cheap grades of tag stock will slough or peel from ordinary wear and from the slightest bit of moisture. It pays to buy a good grade of tag stock for map folders, since with reasonable care it may be expected to last from 15 to 30 years. When purchased in quantity, folders ready for use may cost as much as 10 cents apiece, but the price is not high when one considers the cost of a substantial library binding to protect a book or pamphlet. Likewise, 10 cents is cheap protection for maps which retail at anywhere between $5 and $1,000.

More important than the weight and finish of map folders is the chemical content of the paper from which they are made. Most of the better grades of tag stock are made from a combination of jute and chemical wood pulp in varying proportions. The wood pulp is usually prepared by the sulphate process. The finished stock should contain no chemicals, either volatile or fixed, which might react with old paper or ink. The chemicals used in the best grades of tag stock are self-contained (as hydrogen is contained in water) and cannot be transferred to other sheets of paper such as maps. Poor grades of tag stock, on the other hand, sometimes have free sulphates in their composition (due to improper mixing, washing or bleaching) which are transferable, and which, by uniting with the iron in old ink, produce sulphides. The latter in turn darken the old paper and make it brittle. Therefore it is not good economy to buy a cheap grade of tag stock for map folders. If it is necessary to economize, it is much safer to buy one hundred per cent Manila paper, which is at least safe, though less substantial.

When selecting a size of map folders it is a good plan to allow an inch of clearance on either side between the edge of the folder and the side of the drawer, and at least one inch of clearance at the front; in other words, folders should be two inches shorter than the inside length of the drawer and one inch shorter than the drawer from front to back. This clearance saves the edges of the folders and makes them easier to manipulate. All folders within a drawer should be uniform in size. Small ones in large drawers get pushed back out of sight and temporarily "lost."

Map folders are best filed with the folded edge to the front, since it does not fray or tear so easily as the open edge, and is easier to grasp. With the open edge to the front, it is necessary to hunt out the top and bottom halves of the same folder before pulling it out of the drawer, thus involving a substantial loss of time. Moreover, as most of the dust and dirt that seeps into map drawers enters at the front, the maps themselves are better protected with the fold at the front.

23

A certain amount of information written or printed on each map folder is helpful to the librarian and the reader who may use the collection. Whenever possible it is well to label the folder, giving the name of the author or cartographer, a short title or subject, the place of publication and the date. This information should be placed near the folded edge where it can be read with ease. It is well to choose one corner for labeling, so that the information will always appear in the same position on each folder, a procedure which is even more important on the broad surface of map folders than it is on a 3×5 card.

A most satisfactory apparatus for lettering map folders is the Leroy Scriber and Lettering Template, manufactured by Keuffel & Esser Co., of New York. The scriber, which is a highly specialized penholder and pen, is made in an adjustable form so that it is possible to produce italics as well as straight letters. The template, which regulates the size and shape of the letters and other characters, is made in various sizes. The standard template contains the alphabet and a comma (which may be used as an apostrophe as well) on one side, and 10 numerals, an equality sign (which also serves as a hyphen) and quotation marks on the other. Additional characters are furnished on demand, for an additional charge. A template with parentheses, square brackets and a question mark, for example, is excellent for library work. The Leroy apparatus is easy to operate, and requires very little practice. The spacing of letters and words is the only part of the labeling process which is not mechanically adjusted. Best results will be obtained by using black India (waterproof) ink. With this kind of ink, care should be taken to keep the pens clean; otherwise it is impossible to produce sharp lines of regular width, or

24

to make the ink flow freely. Pens should be cleaned immediately after using with a dilute solution of ammonia (ammonium hydroxide). If the ink is allowed to dry on the pen for several hours, it may be necessary to soak the pen in full strength ammonia overnight, rinsing finally with hot water.

OVERSIZE MAPS

Regardless of how well planned it is, a map collection is likely to have in it some maps which must be cut or folded because of their size. If the librarian or curator in charge is an orthodox antiquarian, he will find it difficult to bring himself to the point of cutting a map, even to make it fit a drawer in which it would be better preserved. On the other hand, the process of folding and unfolding, as everyone knows, soon wears a map at the folds, and it is only a matter of time before they give way entirely, leaving the map in pieces. It is then necessary to hinge the map at the folds or splice the parts with some sort of mending tape. The result is not always satisfactory, and the map is often weakened at the point of the mend. Meanwhile, place names or other important geographical details at the folds have been frayed to the point of obliteration. It is better, then, to cut the map first, carefully and with a sharp knife, and then hinge it with strong mending tape. A hinge should be made so that there is space enough between the two halves to permit folding without friction or overlapping of the edges. A mounted map should always be sectioned before it is folded; otherwise the stresses at the fold between the map and the material on which it is mounted, are very injurious to the map, much more so than a simple fold is to an unmounted one.

SMALL MAPS

It is poor economy to file a map measuring 6×9 inches in a folder measuring 30×38 inches. However, in every collection there will be a certain number of small maps which are important, and yet not large enough to warrant a place in a large folder, stored among large maps. The solution here suggested for the storage of small maps has been tried at the Clements Library and has proved very successful. Letter file boxes of heavy pasteboard were made up, measuring $14 \times 18 \times 3$ inches on the inside. This size was selected because it was found that most of the maps which are smaller than folio size had once been a part of a quarto or octavo atlas. Folders to fit these boxes are made from the cleanest halves of large discarded folders. These are labeled with the cartographer, a short title, place of publication and the date, the date appearing next to the right-hand corner of the folder at the front. The file is arranged in straight chronological order, regardless of subject or area. "SMALL MAPS" is stamped in the upper right corner of the catalogue cards for these maps, to remind the searcher that they may be found under *date* in the file boxes. A leather back strip on each box improves the appearance, and a temporary label (the collection is growing rapidly), bearing the inclusive dates to be found in each box, tells all that is necessary to know about the contents. Each box contains about 50 maps. At the present time there are about 500 small maps in the collection; by filing them as noted above, about 20 large drawers which formerly contained maps of all sizes have been made available for large maps. At the same time these 500 maps occupy only about three cubic feet of space. The system can be expanded indefinitely, and a bookcase or stack range of ordinary size, and not less than

26

14 inches deep, would accommodate several thousand maps without crowding. Any shifting or crumpling can be avoided by packing each box rather closely, so that pressure from both sides will keep the maps rigid within their folders.

II.

CLASSIFICATION

It is assumed in this discussion of the problems associated with the grouping and filing of related map material that the classified map file is to be supplemented by a card catalogue with adequate author (cartographer), title and subject entries. With these two aids in mind—a classified map file arranged according to a plan and a card catalogue which analyzes classes and subclasses and brings out in added entries special features and information which may be found on the maps—two general methods of classification are possible.

The first, which has been adopted by some map collections, is to classify and file according to subject rather than area. That is to say, all railroad maps, all sea charts, all road maps, all topographic surveys would be grouped together under those heads. Under the class *Road Maps* would be found road maps of any part of the world, and under *Charts* would be found charts of all bodies of water, regardless of their geographic location. Subclasses would sort out the road maps of France from those of America or Australia, charts of the North Sea from charts of the Black Sea. This system of classification, however, presupposes considerable geographic and cartographic knowledge on the part of the librarian; and even supposing the librarian or curator were familiar with the fine points which distinguish a general map from a topographic map, a sea chart from an oceanographic survey, there are too many borderline and overlapping classes in the field of *old* maps to make the system practicable. Old maps usually incorporate several subjects, as the term is used above. Prior to the development of highly specialized maps and atlases, when a geographic map of a region was all-embracing in scope, a single map of a state or province might contain, besides the political boundaries, an inset city plan, an elevation of a building, the text of an Indian treaty, the roads, rivers and mountains, in short, all the known physical features of the region. Furthermore, most of the questions which arise in connection with old maps relate first to geographic or political *areas* and secondly to details of those areas. Few questions are asked in which a detached geographic feature or subject such as navigable rivers or mountains is concerned, without reference to the geographic or political area of which such features are a part.

The second method is to classify maps according to area. A map classification based on geographic and political areas is simple to arrange, and can be applied to the largest collections without difficulty. This statement is supported by the practice followed by the Division of Maps of the Library of Congress, where a million and a half maps are classified according to a system based primarily on geographic and political areas. Before assigning area classification headings to a collection of old maps, we should consider the subdivisions of the world which were in use among geographers and map makers before the year 1800, for without an appreciation of the scope of the subject at the time the maps were made, it is impossible to classify such a collection logically and to the best advantage. We find that the pattern of geographical and political subdivisions during the first three hundred years of map printing remained standard—almost universally so. The world was subdivided geographically into the Eastern and Western hemispheres, Europe, Asia and Africa, and was further subdivided, after geographical exploration had proved their existence, into North America, South America and Australia. Oceans and rivers form other geographic groups. Most of the smaller units of the world were presented in the form of political areas, since map units based on climatic or other natural phenomena were almost unheard of. The old method of mapping political areas was not only standard for the regional mapping of the world; it was also borne out in the cosmographic and philosophic "descriptions" which often accompanied the maps, especially maps in atlases. The classification of the collection according to area, then, should be built around this ancient way of subdividing the world, the classification devised by the persons who made the maps. There will be a few exceptions, as in the case of Halley's chart of the world, which was made specifically to demonstrate his new theory of the variations of the compass. Occasionally a map was made for the express purpose of demonstrating the topography of a region or some political phenomena which would demand something more than a "general" classification heading, but in most instances old maps are easily classified under geographic or political headings. They certainly do not warrant a classification based on special subjects which are functions, in an algebraic sense, of a geographic or political area.

A noteworthy exception to the rule of classifying maps according to area may be made in the case of maps which originally accompanied documents and which will be used primarily in conjunction with those documents. The maps in the U. S. Archives, for example, are largely departmental collections containing illustrative material for government treaties, boundary disputes, land grants and other negotiations involving the use of geographic data. These maps were separated from the written or printed documents to facilitate storage and the specialized administration they require. Separate storage, incidentally, makes the material available for general reference as well. U. S. Archival maps, then, are stored first as departmental units and then according to the special subject to which they refer. This functional, or subject classification is wholly justified and most efficient for this type of collection, where data on geographic area, per se, are of secondary or incidental importance.

Although an orderly, well-defined system of classification for the map collection should be established at the outset, a certain amount of latitude in the selection of class headings is recommended. The cataloguer should keep in mind the function of the collection and the readers who will use it. Readers who consult old maps are usually interested in confirming or supplementing textual data. They are interested in either a minute point such as the location of a city, river, fort, the spelling of a place name, or they are interested in compiling all available information relating to an area *during a period of time*. A scholar who is studying the history of the province of Georgia wants to see every map of the area made during the period on which he is working. He is interested in changes in the boundaries and in the outlines of smaller political subdivisions. He wants to trace the development of the road system and the location of taverns, estates, meeting houses and fortified points. A comparative study of a representative collection of maps of the area will furnish the reader with an excellent cross section of the region. In order to facilitate a comparative study of this sort, it is essential that all maps of the *area* be filed together.

Many of the problems which arise in connection with map classification are the result of attempts to apply complicated symbols to material for which they were not designed. With map administration still in the experimental stage, a great deal of confusion can be avoided if symbols are omitted from the classification scheme. Well-defined geographic or political areas are themselves symbols, as much so as a series of decimals; moreover, the possible subdivisions of a geographic area, such as North America, are limited by custom in map making and by long-established political units in a way which all but eliminates the possibility of confusion.

Human knowledge, the record of which is set down in printed books, is constantly expanding; each path has many ramifications which require a system of classification capable of keeping pace with new ideas and new fields of endeavor. The field of maps, on the other hand, is limited by the earth, "theater of human endeavor," which has definite boundaries and a limited number of practical subdivisions. Therefore, keep the map classification as simple as possible. Do not subclassify unless it is convenient to do so. Base the headings of subclasses on the material to be subdivided, whether or not these headings follow the previously selected pattern. If a group of maps does not fit into the classification pattern, do not blame the maps. Make class headings clearly descriptive of the material filed under those heads, striving to make them all-inclusive and at the same time limited in scope. Maps of North America printed before 1800, for example, fall into three groups. First there are general maps of North America, usually including the West Indies. Second, there are maps of the British Dominion in North America published before 1783 which include only the region east of the Mississippi River. The third group consists of maps of the French Dominion which lay west of the Mississippi River. By subdividing maps of North America into these three groups, (1) North America, general, (2) North America, east of the Mississippi, (3) North America, west of the Mississippi, the headings become inclusive and yet limited in scope.

Every collection includes a few items which do not fit well into the previously-selected classification system. Among these oddities are celestial charts and maps of the Northern and Southern hemispheres. The latter, constructed on a polar projection with the north or south pole, as the case may be, at the center and the equator at the periphery, include parts of the eastern and western hemispheres and parts of the continents as well. In order to assign an all-inclusive heading to these maps, they must be classified as world maps, unless the cataloguer decides to assign them their specific headings at the outset. When it comes to filing them, however, it will probably be found most convenient to include them with world maps. Likewise, celestial charts may be filed in the same category. No matter where these geographic oddities are located, proper references in the catalogue will guide the reader to what he wants.

In a growing collection, limited filing space may make it necessary to assign temporary class headings which are not so specific as might be desired. For example, a general heading such as Southern States may be used temporarily for a group of maps including the areas of Kentucky, Louisiana, Georgia and Florida. Later, when space permits, and the number of maps of each of these states makes it necessary, the group can be readily subdivided and filed under headings which are more specific. Headings on the cards meanwhile would refer the reader to the group classification.

Often there is a choice between two or more classification headings under which a map may properly be filed, any one of which would place the map with more or less related material. This problem arises in connection with old charts of the Atlantic Ocean. Most of these are laid down on the same general plan, and include not only the Atlantic Ocean, but also the entire western coast of Europe and the eastern coast of America. There are then three choices of a classification, any of which would be correct. The selection should be made according to the uses of the collection, and the relative importance of the three geographical features in a given locality. In a collection of Americana, the coast of America would be of greater interest to the reader than the coast of Europe or the ocean. On the other hand, in a European map collection, undoubtedly the coastline of Europe should be emphasized. In a collection of marine material, the item would probably be featured as a sea chart, and would be classified under charts of the Atlantic Ocean, following the subject stressed in the title. But in any case, cross references should be made on the catalogue cards, making the chart available for reference under three headings.

Within each class, file first chronologically and then alphabetically, by author or title within the year.

SPECIAL COLLECTIONS

In special collections of maps, there will be some items for which it will be logical to create a class which does not fit in the classification system, but which best describes the material, and at the same time anticipates its uses. For example, in the Clements Library there is a collection of 20 maps filed in a separate drawer next to one containing general maps of Virginia. The classification, YORKTOWN, was selected because the maps refer chiefly to the siege of Yorktown in 1781, even though some of them depict the area within a 20-mile radius of the city. Short titles on the map folders give more specific information to those interested in other features of the region, and complete titles on the catalogue cards tell the rest.

Do not hesitate to assign a class heading that seems a little unorthodox, if it is the one which will best describe the maps which are filed under it. An example is found in eighteenth-century maps of New York which fall into two general groups: (1) those which delineate the entire Province as it was at the time, and (2) those which feature Manhattan Island, and very little else. Another group, which demands some special attention in a large collection, features the Hudson River. These are based on early surveys which give the shore line in some detail, as well as the soundings of the channel. Class headings for New York maps, then, may logically combine both political and geographic subdivisions.

OBSOLETE POLITICAL AREAS

Maps of obsolete political areas are common. They should be classified under the heading which comes the closest to describing the actual geographical area represented on the map itself. Maps of the Connecticut Reserve, for example, depict an area lying along the south shore of Lake Erie which is obsolete, and which is at present unrelated to the state of Connecticut. In selecting a classification for such maps, the area and not the title should receive primary consideration. The best class here may be OHIO or LAKE ERIE, depending on the classification headings already established. Adequate cross references in the card catalogue are of course essential to the treatment of obsolete political areas.

REPRODUCTIONS

Reproductions of old maps should be classified and catalogued as though they were originals. The publication data referring to the reproduction should be noted on the catalogue card, but should not influence the classification of the map, or the information lettered on the map folder.

Both facsimiles and forgeries are reproductions, of different sorts, which attempt to reproduce faithfully an original in all its details, but the latter also attempt to deceive. Only with experience can one expect to become proficient in detecting map forgeries, but it is fortunately true that a little experience will go a long way towards making the librarian familiar with the "feel" of old paper and the marks characteristic of the engraver's burin. The general appearance of a genuine map as opposed to the smooth look of the forgery will be enough to help the librarian avoid most pitfalls. If a rare map is appraised by an inexperienced librarian who contemplates its purchase, and there is very much money involved, it is best to consult an expert, who can usually detect a forgery, and who may even know the origin of the perpetration. The best forgers are well known ("by their works ye shall know them").

III.

CATALOGUING

THE AUTHOR, *i.e.*, THE CARTOGRAPHER

Every map, like every book and every other product of creative effort, has an author: a person or persons responsible for the existence of the work. Unlike the author of a book, who transfers ideas to paper by means of words, the cartographer is responsible for a picture, the reproduction of a situation. The picture may portray the topography of a piece of land, the soundings of a harbor, the plan of a city, or the size and relative positions of the celestial bodies. The picture may have double significance, as when roads or navigable rivers are superimposed on a topographical picture of a region. Always, however, there is a picture, and always there is a cartographer responsible for that picture.

Who is the cartographer or map maker? Before attempting to answer this question, we should bear in mind certain facts relative to the history of cartography, facts which make the determination of map authorship a different problem from that of the authorship of a printed book. Map making is closely related to the pictorial or "fine" arts, whose history is very different from that of the printed book. A different technique is employed in map engraving, a technique which early established it as a separate craft, and at the same time had much to do with widening the separation between the processes of bookmaking and map making.

When there is no definite statement as to the cartographer on the map itself, the cataloguer must either try to interpret what information is available on the map in an effort to determine who was the cartographer, or he may waive the problem and enter the map under some other heading, such as the title or general subject. On modern maps the problem of authorship is solved in part by copyright laws, but thousands of old maps were made without the protection of such laws.

Prior to the invention of lithography (1796–98), engraving was the chief method used to reproduce and print maps. Wood, copper, silver, and later steel, were the chief materials employed in the process. Copper was perhaps the most widely used. It was very expensive and hard to get, and the transfer of a drawing from paper to metal was a long, slow process. Of necessity, craftsmen became very skilful at altering copper plates. And the amazing adaptability of a copper plate increases the problem of determining the cartographer of an old map, when his name and function are not specifically mentioned on the map itself.

There is ample evidence to prove that many map plates had long and checkered careers. They were borrowed, begged and stolen; they were patched, spliced, added to, erased and otherwise altered until their original owners would never have recognized them. Maps have been found which were made of two plates, one ten years older than the other. Many are known whose titles were altered or completely changed, with the names of new cartographers replacing those of the original creators. In some instances such alterations were legitimate, but in many others it was undoubtedly a matter of plagiarism. Map men seem to have been very temperamental; they would work together for a time and then suddenly denounce their partners in print as thieves and ingrates, each accusing the other of horrible crimes. Then we find that the quarrelsome partners collaborated on a new map or series of maps a few years later. The cataloguer should remember that for every survey made in Europe prior to the nineteenth century which resulted in a map, there were a hundred derivatives in the form of copies, enlargements, reductions and plagiarisms.

In many cases there was little honor among the gentry who made maps prior to the nineteenth century, and yet there was among them considerable publishing zeal and professional jealousy. Either of these factors is strong enough to account for the ungentlemanly practices encountered in the history of early cartography. Tracing the original cartographer, then, involves some knowledge of early map makers and their ways, information that may not be readily available to all who are faced with the problem of making a catalogue of a map collection.

During the first three centuries of map engraving, accurate geographic information was hard to get. Travel was a hazardous business, and the mobility of map makers was limited by expensive and unreliable transportation. For this reason, publishers were obliged to coöperate to a certain extent, in order to supply the public with the latest maps of different parts of the world. It was a common practice for surveyors of different countries to make maps of the area closest at hand and then exchange their work with the surveyors of other regions. While one man was surveying the

coast of France, another might be making a survey of
the city of London. It was profitable for the two map
makers to exchange productions and to share with one
another the all too few scraps of accurate data concerning the geography of the known world, at the
same time increasing their stock in trade. Centers of
publishing and engraving were widely scattered. Surveys were made in Italy and engraved in Holland.
Dutch cartographers worked in England; French cartographers worked in Italy and Holland. Ideas and
copper plates went back and forth across Europe and
across the English Channel. The titles and legends on
maps were frequently changed (also the language of
the map) to fit the occasion and place of publication.
Maps were copied with and without the permission of
the cartographers; copies resulted so like the original
that only an expert can tell the difference, although
the dates of publication were ten years apart.

A great many maps were printed during the first
three centuries of map making, but the cataloguer will
soon discover that old maps of certain areas fall into
groups which bear a striking family resemblance to
one another, though they vary individually. The answer is that there was usually a fundamental map,
made perhaps from an original survey, after which
others were patterned in the ways mentioned above.
The information on a given map may be vastly different from that found on its prototype, but the cataloguer should recognize the possibility of an earlier attempt, and hesitate before attributing an early map to
a cartographer without sufficient evidence to support
the claim. When there is any doubt, enter the map
under some head other than the cartographer, or at
least query the name entered as cartographer. A similarity of pattern and area does not prove identical

authorship. It is extremely interesting and enlightening, however, to track down the prototype of a series of maps, noting the changes that have been made in the original over a period of years. By this means the cataloguer can trace the progress, and in some cases the retrogression of geographical knowledge of given parts of the world. (Many false rumors and geographic data were incorporated on early maps, often remaining there for a painfully long time.)

Finished maps are usually the product of many minds, even though the authorship may rightly be attributed to one or two persons. Whereas some map makers were able to get into the field and actually survey an area, many more had to draw their maps from the observations and field notes of others. In the production of a map there are usually six steps involved. These should be considered at this time, because: each step may be represented by a personal name on the finished map; any personal name, although not that of the cartographer, may supply a clue which will lead ultimately to the determination of the cartographer, the place of publication and the date; every personal name representing any one of the six steps contributes a fragment towards the whole mass of information which will one day become shaped into an adequate history of cartography. The steps involved are as follows:

(1) *Making the Survey.* After the area to be surveyed is decided upon, a point of departure is selected; the position of that point is found by astronomical observation, as accurately as available instruments will allow; a base line is drawn from the point of departure, after which the area is surveyed by one of several techniques. Notes are made, measurements are put down on paper, as well as any other data to be in-

cluded in the survey, such as topographical features: rivers, swamps, cities and roads.

(2) *Making the Finished Draft.* From the field notes of the surveyor, the actual map is drawn. If it is to be a finished plan of permanent value, professing a certain degree of accuracy, a scale is selected by the draftsman; for example, one inch on the map may equal 500 yards of the survey, and the final drawing is made to that scale.

(3) *Preparation for Reproduction.* The finished draft, if it is to be made available to the public in more than one or two copies, is next transferred or copied on a hard surface. It may be engraved or etched on a plate of copper, steel or wood; it may be laid down on a specially prepared stone (lithography). From this prepared plate or stone, many copies can be reproduced.

(4) *Printing.* The engraved plate is next fixed in a press, and the plate is inked. A sheet of paper is pressed against the inked plate, thereby producing an impression or copy. As many copies are "pulled" or "struck off" as the publisher thinks the market will bear.

(5) *Publishing.* The publisher of a work is the financial backer of the enterprise; he may furnish the money for making the survey and supervise every step in the production. On the other hand he may furnish only the ink, paper and press on which the job is to be printed. But he is always an important factor (really the promoter) in the process of map making. He universally demands recognition, if not the lion's share of the profits. Some editors and publishers of old maps claimed authorship, as well as ownership, of all maps financed by them. Others were very conscientious about acknowledging the actual cartog-

rapher, even if they did not allow him to share in the profit—when there was any.

(6) *Selling.* Prior to the nineteenth century the function of the book and map seller was more closely associated with the printing and publishing trade than it is today; in fact there were many men who were printer-publisher-sellers. When the publishing and selling were represented by two different individuals, there was sometimes an agreement whereby the vendor's name was printed on the map, as well as his place of business. In other instances publishers listed several places where the map could be purchased, and the names of the sellers who were authorized to handle them. The function of the map vendor is stressed here because his name is sometimes conspicuous on the printed map, and his place should neither be ignored nor overemphasized. He may be *only* the seller, but again he may be the cartographer, printer and publisher, as well as the purveyor of the finished article.

The original surveyor did not always make the final draft; the delineator (draftsman) did not always do the engraving; the engraver was not always the publisher. But there is, at one extreme, the case of the cartographer John Fitch, who executed every step in the production of his map of the Northwest with his own hands, even to the peddling of the finished product. At the other extreme there are instances where every step in the production was done by a different person. Sometimes only the surveyor's name appears on the map; sometimes only the publisher's; but there are other times when the names of the surveyor, the copyist, the engraver, the printer, the publisher and the book and print dealer commissioned to sell the map, all appear on the finished map. These details may not seem extremely important, but they should be considered before one assumes too hastily that because a man's name appears on a map, he is the cartographer.

From among the personal names appearing on the map, we must find the cartographer, if possible. And in most cases we must depend entirely on the map itself for the desired information. If the title states, or if the statement is made anywhere else on the map, that the map is *by* a person, we must assume that that person is the cartographer, even though there is reason to doubt the assertion. "After the surveys of . . ." is another phrase which implies authorship, even though another name appears on the map as draftsman or delineator (sometimes following the personal name as *delineavit, del., delin.,* or *fecit*). The Latin noun *auctore,* sometimes abbreviated to *auc.* or *auct.,* following a personal name, implies the cartographer. However, the terms *scripsit* or *scrip.; sculp.* or *sculpsit; pinxt* or *pinxit; delin.,* and *fecit (fec.)* are indefinite, and are used interchangeably, sometimes referring to the draftsman or copyist, sometimes to the engraver and sometimes to the cartographer.

The temptation to use a Latin title was too much for some people, and the above terms were used without a full appreciation of their literal meaning. The term *delineator (delin.* or *del.)* is sometimes confusing. Map makers often produced several maps at a time, compiling the work of subordinates. The job of making the final drawings was turned over to men who did nothing but make fair copies of the original drafts. These copyists were sometimes rewarded for their pains by being allowed to sign their work in very small letters followed by *del.* or *delin.* The delineator, or the man who signs himself as such, is usually this copyist who made the final drawing from which the engraver worked. But there are also instances where the delineator is the cartographer, to whom we must ascribe authorship. Do not assume that the delineator is the cartographer unless his name is repeated in the title or in some other place on the map, followed by a more conclusive statement of authorship

Certain phrases preceding a personal name may be safely interpreted as referring to the cartographer:

1. Made under the direction of . . . .
2. Amended and corrected by . . . . [unless the name of the original author is also given]
3. From the latest observations of/by . . . .
4. Compiled from the latest surveys of . . . .
5. Surveyed in the present year by . . . .

If a map is ascribed to a certain cartographer and has been reissued (1) "Amended and corrected by . . . .," or (2) "With the latest observations of . . . ." another person, authorship still belongs to the individual responsible for the first production.

Study the map carefully before attempting to catalogue it. Do not try to decide who is the cartographer until you have located every personal name printed on the map. These names may be well hidden, and often they must be searched for among the borders or decorations of the margins. If there is any doubt as to the cartographer, after the map has been studied carefully, it is well to enter the map under the title and subject, pending further investigation.

MAP TITLES

The title of an old map, if there is one, may appear scrawled across the top of the map in large, boldface type, or it may be tucked away in a dark corner, almost obliterated by the shading or printing around it. A map title may be incorporated in a long dedica-

tory epistle, such as that for Paxton's map of Philadelphia: *To the citizens of Philadelphia this new plan
of the city and its environs, taken from actual survey
is respectfully dedicated by their humble serv! John
A. Paxton.* There are instances where a map title, the
only appearance of it on the face of the map, is found
in the middle of the note of registration or official
"entry." Such is the case with Reading Howell's map
of Pennsylvania: *District of Pennsylvania, to wit: Be
it remembered, that on the thirteenth day of June, in
the fifteenth year of the Independence of the United
States of America, Reading Howell, of the said district,
hath deposited in this office the title of a map, the
right whereof he claims as author, in the words following, to wit "A map of Pennsylvania, & the parts con-
nected therewith . . . by Reading Howell." In con-
formity to the act of the Congress of the United States.*
. . .

The title of a map used as a frontispiece in a book
may appear not on the map itself, but on the title
page of the book, or on any one of the preliminary
leaves. On some large-scale maps there are two titles,
both of equal value, one describing the right half or
the lower half of the map, and the other describing
the left or upper half, as the case may be. But most
often the title of an old map will be found enclosed
in a cartouche, the nearest approach to a title-page
format to be found in the field of cartography.

The name, principle and use of the cartouche have
become corrupted during the course of time. Scroll-
like figures were used by the Egyptians to enclose inscriptions on tablets and pillars. The volutes of the
Ionian capital are referred to as cartouches. According
to the *Encyclopaedia Britannica,* the cartouche refers
properly to an oval formed by a rope knotted at one

end. This design was originally used to enclose the
arms of the Pope or members of royal families. The
cartouche in its proper form is found on very old
maps, sometimes topped by a cardinal's hat or some
other symbol of the clergy. But as different schools of
engraving sprang up in Europe during the latter part
of the sixteenth century, characterized by new and in-
creasingly ornate designs, the original form of the cartouche underwent remarkable transformations. The
heavy classical scrolls of the sixteenth century Dutch
maps became less formal. Cherubs and garlands of
flowers were added to the cartouche. Lords and ladies
were placed around the scroll; astronomical figures
and scenic views were incorporated in the figure originally devoted to the title alone. During the eighteenth
century the scroll motif was sometimes replaced by
banners, rocks, shields and ribbons, in fact all manner
of designs were tried as a background for the title.
Often a second or even a third cartouche was added to

the map to enclose not only the title, but also the author's name, or the place of publication, or the scale. Sometimes a cartouche was used to enclose a note or legend pertaining to the map.

While discussing the cartouche, it may be well to point out the fact that an elaborate cartouche, while designed primarily to enclose a title, may contain a great deal of additional information, and that this information is frequently inconspicuous, and consequently very easily overlooked. Engravers had a habit of working their initials into the design of the cartouche, using a script almost impossible to detect with the naked eye. The only date on a map may be hidden in the folds of a piece of ribbon draped at the bottom of the cartouche, or partly concealed in some other part of the design. When a copper plate was sold or stolen, it was usually altered somewhat, and dates and authors' names were frequently erased. By examining the cartouche with a magnifying glass, it is sometimes possible to work out an altered date or another author's name.

Titles on old maps vary widely in length and accuracy. Some are short and concise, and give an accurate picture of what one may expect to find on the map. Others are long and rambling, giving not only the title of the map, but a wordy biography of its author and the changes and revisions that have been made in the map, all of which leave the reader with a rather hazy idea of what the map actually portrays. It is well to read every word of these long titles, however, as they frequently contain much information that is useful, and though an author's name may appear on the second line in bold type, fifteen lines later the reader may learn that since the original publication of the map it has been completely revised, redrawn and republished by another person whose name appears in small type on the last line. The following illustrates the complex title sometimes encountered:

A map of South Carolina and a part of Georgia . . . composed from surveys taken by The Hon. William Bull Esq. Lt. Governor, Captain Gascoign, Hugh Bryan, Esq; and William De Brahm Esqr; Surveyor General of the South^n District of North America, republished with considerable additions, from the surveys made & collected by John Stuart Esqr His Majesty's Superintendent of Indian Affairs, by William Faden successor to the late T. Jefferys, Geographer to the King . . .

Many titles do not properly describe the area shown on the map. This is especially true of maps of North America and parts thereof. The title, *A map of the British dominions in North America,* unless the reader is familiar with the phrase, will not give a very clear picture of what the map portrays. For a further discussion of this problem see the section on Classification. Before making a subject card for a map, it is well to check the title, if it is at all descriptive of the contents of the map, with the actual geographical area shown on the map itself. If there is a great deal

of difference between the two, some note to that effect should be made on the catalogue card. Sometimes it is convenient to supply a short sentence in addition to the map title, in square brackets, clarifying the title description.

MAPS WITHOUT TITLES

Any person who handles a collection of old maps of any size will find a certain number without titles. Some of these maps will have authors, in which case the map can be catalogued without difficulty. If the author is not given, the subject entry will be the main entry in the catalogue. But in either case a title should be supplied to explain the subject heading, when the subject is the main entry, or to describe in some detail what the author has done, when his name appears on the map. When a title must be supplied, study the map carefully before attempting to compose a title. Determine the limits of the area shown on the map and plan to include them in the title, north and south, east and west, mentioning any very important features such as the location of a city or fort, or a boundary line within the area. Supplied titles, of course, can never be used for comparing two map entries, because no two persons would interpret the contents of a map, and set down their interpretations on a card, in the very same words. It is well, therefore, to make the title short and concise, relying on subject headings and added entries in the catalogue to bring out more reliable points of comparison.

One of the best illustrations of the problems involved in supplying titles for old maps is a series of charts of the Atlantic coast and harbors. These charts, published between 1774 and 1782 by J. F. W. Des Barres, appear in the atlas known as *The Atlantic*

Neptune. Many of them, though remarkably accurate surveys for the time, were published without titles. Perhaps the author felt that they were clear enough to read without titles. Nineteen copies of this great atlas in the Library of Congress have been collated and carefully analyzed, and titles have been supplied wherever necessary. (Cf. P. Lee Philips, *A list of geographical atlases in the Library of Congress,* v.3 and 4.) A careful study of the supplied titles for these charts will aid the cataloguer in making up titles for other maps and charts.

When two maps or charts cover the same area, or approximately the same, with some overlapping, or when two charts cover the same area, one showing it in greater detail than the other, such data as the size and scale of the map are important points of identification, supplementing the title.

IMPRINTS

The imprint of a map, i.e., the place of publication, the printer or publisher and the date, may be found anywhere on the face of the map, or may be entirely lacking. The place of publication may be in one corner of the map and the date in another, while the publisher's name may be enclosed in an elaborate cartouche containing no other information. In other words, it is often necessary to gather up imprint data before adding it to the catalogue card. It is unusual to find the imprint data closely associated and set down in the usual cataloguing sequence: place, printer or publisher, and date.

When the imprint data are on the map, but scattered, it is good practice to group the information on the catalogue card. When there is any doubt about a place name, publisher or date being associated with the imprinting of the map, the questionable data should be bracketed on the card. For example, "London, Printed by Wm. Faden" may be printed on the map just below the title. The only date may be under the "Dedication," located on some other part of the map. If there seems to be little doubt that the date of the dedication is also that of publication, it may be taken as the date of the map, but should be questioned and should appear in brackets on the card following the rest of the imprint, with a note calling attention to the fact. And if the only clue to the place of publication is the name of the publisher or the street on which his shop is located, the place of publication should be bracketed. In the case of a detailed bibliographical study of a map, it is important to state the location on the map of every bit of data, no matter how scattered. Frequently two issues of the same map vary only in the *location* of the imprint on the map. On one it may be at the top of the map, on a second issue it may be located below the border or under the title cartouche.

When a map has on it two or more imprints, the latest imprint may be taken as the correct one. But regardless of the date of the imprint, one should always be on the lookout for internal evidence of a later date. Oftentimes maps were reissued with new and corrected data without changing the imprint. It is sometimes possible to spot these changes by watching for conspicuous boundary lines, or "Notes" in very small print, announcing the discoveries of an explorer, or the running of a boundary line. Such notes are usually dated.

Do not try to date a map solely by the book or atlas in which it is bound. Maps were used over and over again to illustrate books of travel and to fill out the pages of atlases. Some map plates were in use forty years after their original publication. Maps of the western hemisphere are usually easier to date than those of the eastern hemisphere. The latter remained more or less unchanged for long periods of time, while the former usually boasted the very latest discoveries and the latest geographic data. This is especially true of maps of North America or parts thereof. A knowledge of American history will help the cataloguer at this point.

When a map bears no imprint, examine it closely for internal evidence that will furnish a clue as to where it was published and when. Note carefully the

language of the map and the language of the title. They may not be the same. Note the decorations on the map; the coats of arms, and the dedication, if there is one. The king or other royal personage to whom the map is dedicated will often help to date the map within limits, and will usually have a bearing on the place of publication. Note whether the map was published with the "privilege" of a monarch, according to an act of Parliament, or an act of Congress. There is often a statement telling where the prime meridian of longitude was laid down, and if there is no such statement on the map, the numbering of the meridians will indicate the point of departure. French cartographers often took their prime meridian through Paris; London was often the prime meridian used by English cartographers. American map makers used various places according to their tastes, before Greenwich was settled upon as the standard point of departure, and if Philadelphia or Washington was selected as the prime meridian, the chances are the map was printed and published in America.

Internal evidence will help in narrowing the upper and lower date limits between which the map was published. If reference books are not available, study the political boundaries carefully. Watch for "newly established colonies" and the tracks of explorers, which will help to establish a lower date limit for the publication. Maps of North America printed between 1775 and 1783 often have on them some reference to a battle or campaign. It is safe to say that Revolutionary maps were published as soon after a battle took place as possible, usually within a year, as such maps were in great demand in Europe by officials of all nations. If the map maker has a note on the map to the effect that he has used the maps of Fry & Jefferson and

Lewis Evans to compile his survey, the statement will give a clue to the lower limit of the date, as it is possible to find the dates of both of these important maps. Watermarks are sometimes helpful aids to dating old maps, especially when a date has been incorporated in the design of the watermark, but dated paper is not always trustworthy. Enterprising publishers (and sometimes forgers) have been known to reprint an old map on old, dated paper, to give the reproduction an appearance of antiquity. Moreover there are instances where maps on dated paper have been used several years after their original appearance, in atlases or as illustrations in printed books, bearing data which belie the dated watermark and the publication date as well.

Unless good reference tools are available, the whole process of supplying imprint data must be one of deduction based on internal evidence found on the map itself. The correct interpretation of such evidence requires experience and study, but lack of these qualifications should not discourage the map cataloguer. It is always possible to go back and revise, if necessary.

DETERMINATION OF MAP SIZES: THE COLLATION

The size of the map and the information as to where it is to be found, i.e., *In, With,* or *From* a book or atlas, constitutes the collation and should be set down on the collation line below the imprint. In recording the size of a map there is a choice of using either the metric system or the English linear system of measurement. The chief point in favor of the English linear system is that most of the important bibliographic guides and check lists of maps and atlases use it, beginning with the various publications compiled under the direction of P. Lee Philips and issued by the Library of Congress (*see* Bibliography). As these works will remain standard references for many years to come, it seems most convenient to follow the example of the Library of Congress in this matter. It may be argued that the metric system gives a finer measurement, but it will be pointed out below that fine measurements in dealing with old maps are useless gestures.

Give the measurement of the map in inches to the nearest eighth of an inch giving the vertical dimen-

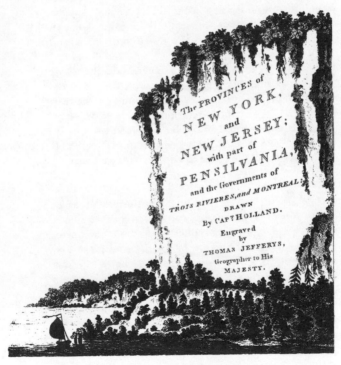

The PROVINCES of
NEW YORK,
and
NEW JERSEY;
with part of
PENSILVANIA,
and the Governments of
TROIS RIVIERES, and MONTREAL;
DRAWN
By Cap? HOLLAND.
Engraved
by
THOMAS JEFFERYS,
Geographer to His
MAJESTY.

sion first. Take the measurements of the map from *the extreme edge of the outside border line* on one side to the corresponding point on the opposite side. A fixed rule is necessary here as the border lines on old maps are sometimes as wide as a quarter of an inch.

Many old copper plates were not cut squarely, nor were the borders or neat lines made square, hence the width of a map may vary as much as a quarter of an inch, depending on whether the width is measured across the top or across the bottom. Consequently, it is obvious that an attempt to get the measurement in fractions smaller than eighths of an inch would be utterly impractical. For a preliminary examination or consideration of a map, the approximate size noted on the catalogue card, to the nearest eighth of an inch, is enough to give the reader an idea whether or not the map is worth looking at; for a bibliographic comparison of two copies of the same map, a side by side study is indicated, and at that point size does not weigh so heavily as other evidence which will be available in an actual comparison of the two copies.

The amount of shrinkage found in specimens of old paper varies widely. The paper was usually dampened for printing, and variations in the "wetness" would effect the size of the printed area on the sheet after drying. Shrinkage is affected in some cases by the weight of the paper. The atmospheric changes to which the map is subjected from time to time also play an important role in paper shrinkage. Shrinkage is sometimes great in one direction and almost imperceptible in the other. These facts should be kept in mind when comparing the size of two copies of the same map.

There will be cases where the above rules for measuring a map cannot apply, and when a departure from the rule is necessary, a note to that effect should follow the actual measurements. For example:

(1) When there is no neat line or definite border line from which to take a measurement, the plate mark—the impression made in the paper by the plate at the time of printing—may be used. In this case the words *plate mark* or *plate size* should follow the dimensions. When maps are mounted on board or heavy cloth, the plate mark is often pressed out and cannot be seen with the naked eye, and is therefore of no help. In most cases, however, some trace of the plate mark is visible.

(2) Some maps have a heavily decorated border, or an irregular scalloped edge. This is especially true of maps printed in the early part of the nineteenth century. In such cases the outer edge of the border cannot be used for getting the size of the map. Here it is necessary for the cataloguer to select the most practical line within the irregular border, and from it take the size, noting on the card as clearly, but as briefly as possible, from what point the size was taken.

(3) When a map is in two or more sheets, or when a map has been cut into sections and mounted, with space between each section, proper allowance should of course be made when taking measurements.

(4) Photostats will cause some trouble unless the exact scale of the reproduction is known. If the photostat has been made to full scale, the size of the map may be taken directly from the photostat as the size of the actual map. But if the photostat is at all reduced from the size of the original, the amount of reduction should always be considered in the measurements. If the photostat is poor, or if there is an unequal amount of shrinkage in the sheets which compose it, the size of

the map should be obtained from the owner of the original. The same is true of photostats which have been pasted together. For the sake of accuracy, it is best to have the measurements of the original.

A simple yet effective check can be made on the scale of a photostatic copy of a map by having two six-inch rulers photographed with the original map. If one ruler is laid along the wide margin and the other along the long margin, the slightest error in the scale of the finished reproduction can be detected.

(5) When a great deal of information appears outside the limits of the map proper, such as a running title, the imprint, or several lines of letterpress, there is sometimes doubt as to how much besides the map proper should be included in the measurements of the map. For the sake of uniformity, it is best to adhere to the rule of measuring the limits of the map proper, which limits are usually bounded by a ruled line or lines. This procedure should be followed even when the title is outside the border lines.

(6) Maps of the world or of the two hemispheres are often found printed as one or two circles, without the usual rectangular shaped neat lines enclosing them. If the map is one circle, take the diameter of the circle as the size and note the fact after the actual measurement on the card. If the hemispheres or circular world are enclosed by a neat line, take the measurements as though the map were rectangular in shape.

(7) Some maps, and especially manuscript maps, will have no borders at all. If the sheet on which the map is drawn is well filled, it will do no harm to give the size of the sheet as the size of the map. If, on the other hand, the actual drawing occupies only a small part of the sheet, a rough measurement of the actual drawing will be of some value, and will not be so mis-

AMSTELODAMI,
Excudebat Ioannes
Ianßonius.

GRANATA NOVA
ET CALIFORNIA.

leading as though the size of the entire sheet were given. The aim should be to give the reader as accurate a picture as possible of what he may expect to see when he goes to the map itself.

If the map is in any but the usual sheet form, and is therefore to be found in some unusual storage place, such as a locked case or range, or among "small maps," mention of the fact may be made either in the collation or on the back of the card.

NOTES AND ADDED ENTRIES

The body of the catalogue card should include only the name and dates of the cartographer, the title, imprint and the collation. This leaves considerable information to be set down on the card in the form of notes. At this point the problem arises as to how far the cataloguer should go in making notes, and how exhaustive the notes should be. It is futile and unnecessary to try to exhaust on the catalogue card all available data relating to each map. Limited space makes it imperative to select with care only the most vital data for inclusion on the catalogue card. In the interests of efficiency notes should be as concise as possible. Although extension cards are sometimes indicated, it is advisable to limit each map entry to one card. Readers usually prefer to consult the map itself rather than read through two or three catalogue cards, especially when they are not printed. (See Sheet Catalogues.)

The type of notes selected for inclusion on the card will vary with the collection and with the type of questions asked by investigators using the catalogue and the collection. These factors will also influence the number and kind of added entries to be made for each map. Some cataloguers will choose to stress biblio-

61

graphic data such as printers, publishers, delineators and engravers, while others will consider geographic data such as scale, projection and prime meridia of foremost importance.

The order in which notes should be set down on the card is debatable, but for the sake of uniformity, some order should be established and adhered to. Among the numerous data which merit the attention of the map cataloguer, the following are important:

(1) *Scale.*

Any map which makes a pretense of being accurate is drawn to scale. The scale of a map is the key to, and is defined as, "the relative proportion of the linear dimensions of the parts of a map to the dimensions of the corresponding parts of the earth." Modern maps are projected on carefully computed scales, every effort being made to eliminate all variables, such as paper shrinkage, which would detract from the accuracy of the finished product. Most old maps were not so carefully made, and are not often trustworthy documents from which to take measurements. They are often

compilations based on maps or surveys made by several different individuals at different times and under different working conditions. We have a right to assume that the accuracy of map makers was a variable factor prior to the year 1800, even more than it is today. For one thing, surveying instruments were less precise. Therefore, in a compiled survey made up of several contributions, small regional surveys, for example, the variable factor of accuracy is multiplied considerably, and should be taken into consideration by anyone consulting early maps or trying to catalogue them. Likewise, the accuracy of the scale varies widely, and the cataloguer or reader using old maps should not expect too much from the bar scale computed and printed 150 or 250 years ago.

The scale of the map should constitute the first "note" on the card. When setting down the scale, use the phraseology found on the map, such as "American miles 69 1/2 to a Degree [the length of the mile] or 10 Miles to an Inch." This quotation, besides giving the scale of the map, furnishes a bibliographic "point" which may be important in differentiating two editions of a map: the scale was often changed as well as the imprint, when a map was reëdited or republished.

Unfortunately only a small proportion of old maps are laid down on a scale computed in such simple units as miles to an inch or feet to an inch. Among the units of linear measure found on old maps are leagues, English leagues, Spanish leagues, perches, chains and arpents. As yet there is no table which will enable the cataloguer to convert all possible units of linear measure to a common factor such as feet or miles, but the table under "Measure" in Webster's *New International Dictionary*, 2d ed., is helpful. Better still is the *International Critical Tables of Numerical Data* . . .

prepared by the National Research Council, New York [etc.] 1926–30. A third source of information, now in preparation, is the table compiled by S. W. Boggs, for the express purpose of converting map scales into a common unit of measure. When published, this will be an invaluable aid both to geographers and librarians.

Natural scale, i.e., the relative proportion of a linear unit on the map to the same unit on the earth's surface (1:500,000) is most commonly used today. The natural scale, also called fractional scale ($\frac{1}{500,000}$) was probably never employed in map making prior to 1800; at least it was never set down as such, although there is little doubt that it entered into the computations of the more scientific cartographers.

A valuable aid to the determination of the natural scale of maps is the *Natural Scale Indicator,* an ingenious device prepared by S. W. Boggs in the Office of the Geographer, U. S. Department of State, and printed by the U. S. Geological Survey, Department of the Interior. It may be used "(1) To ascertain the natural scale of any map on which parallels of latitude, or one or more graphic scales of linear distances, are shown; (2) To lay out a graphic linear scale, either in kilometers, statute miles, or feet, for any map of known natural scale." The device, consisting of a strip of cardboard graduated into four scales, is extremely versatile and easy to operate.

(2) *Projection.*

Map making involves the reproduction of some part of the earth on a plane surface, i.e., a sheet of paper. If the true relationship of all points involved in the transfer is to be maintained, distortion of the *shape* of the area on paper is necessary. If, on the other hand, an effort is made to preserve the shape of the area to be reproduced, the true relationship between various points, i.e., uniform scale, must be sacrificed.

In the past two thousand years many systems of map projection have been devised, all of which were designed to increase the accuracy of map making, and also to meet the special requirements of different types of surveys. Polar projections, for example, with the north or south pole at the center and the equator at the periphery, were devised to show most clearly the *shape* of the land areas at the northern and southern extremities of the earth. Equal-area projections, on the other hand, ignoring the shape factor, were designed to preserve the *size* of some part of the earth's surface, such as a state or county, while maintaining as nearly as possible all points of the area in their exact relationship, i.e., to scale. Map projection is a technical subject involving the use of higher mathematics. Familiarity with the various systems of projection requires considerable study, and the ability to identify these systems, with their numerous modifications, on sight, is limited to a very few skilled cartographers. It is best therefore to ignore the projection of the map unless it is given on the map, either in the title (e.g., "A map of the world on Mercator's projection") or in a note. If the projection is included on the card, it should follow the scale, either on the same line or the line below.

(3) *The Delineator.*

It has been pointed out that the cartographer and the person who signs himself as the delineator are often two individuals. When this is true, the delineator, who is responsible for the final drawing, should be brought out in a note, either in quotation form or with the personal name followed by a conventional symbol previously decided upon such as (del.). An

TREATMENT OF AN INSET MAP

```
Robert de Vaugondy, Gilles, 1688-1766.
   Les isles Britanniques qui comprennent
les royaumes d'Angleterre, d'Ecosse et
d'Irlande; par le Sr. Robert...[Paris]
1754.
   18 3/4 x 23 in.  (From Robert, G. et
Robert, D.: Atlas universel, Paris, 1757)
   Scale: 28 English miles to an inch.
"Gravé par E. Dussy."
   Inset: Supplément pour les isles Or-
cades, Schetland, et Fero.
```

Main Entry Card of Map Proper

```
        1. British Isles
        2. Ireland
        I. Dussy, E., sculp.

        Inset cataloged
```

Verso of Ma. ntry Card of Map Proper

TREATMENT OF AN INSET MAP

[Robert de Vaugondy, Gilles] 1688-1766.
  Supplément pour les isles Orcades,
Schetland, et Fero.   [Paris, 1754]
  7 1/2 x 7 in. (Inset <u>on</u> Robert, Gilles:
Les isles Britanniques... [Paris] 1754)
  [Engraved by E. Dussy]

Main Entry Card for Inset

1. Orkney Islands
2. Shetland Islands
3. Faroe Islands

Verso of Main Entry Card for Inset

added entry should always be made for the delineator, giving his dates whenever possible.

(4) *The Engraver.*

The name of the engraver is a bibliographic point which deserves a place among the notes. His is an important contribution in the making of the finished product. His name would logically follow the name of the delineator in the notes, either on the same line or directly beneath it, followed by a conventional symbol such as (sculp.). An added entry should be made for every engraver's name appearing on the map. The engraver's dates, or even a *fl.* date, often aid in dating anonymous maps which have little else to contribute in the way of clues.

(5) *The Dedication.*

The dedication of the map, if there is one, is often a source of important information to the cataloguer. The person to whom the map is dedicated may furnish a clue to the circumstances surrounding the making of the map, the country it was made in, and the approximate date of the publication. The person who signs the dedication is usually the cartographer, although he may be the editor or publisher. In the case of a dated dedication, one may be sure that publication followed closely, but it is not safe to date a map solely from the date of the dedication. Maps were sometimes republished from five to ten years after the dedication was signed and dated, without changing the latter. Do not ignore the dedication, however; it may contain important though wordy information. Make the dedication note as brief as possible, including only the essential parties involved: "To Henry Bouquet . . . Henry Dawkins." The same general rules apply to the "privilege" notices which appeared on many maps published prior to the eighteenth cen-

FORM OF ENTRY USED FOR A DEDICATION

```
Price, Charles.
  A new and correct map of the world
projected upon the plane of the hori-
zon... by C. Price.   [London] 1714.
  24 3/4 x 39 in.
  No scale indicated.
  "H: Jerasson, delin, et Sculp, London."
  Dedication: To His Grace Charles Duke
of Shrewsbury [Chas. Talbot]...C. Price"
  "Sold by G. Willdey at the Great Toy
Shop..."
```

Main Entry Card

```
        1. Mappemonde
        I. Jerasson, H., sculp.
       II. Willdey, George
      III. Talbot, Charles, Duke of
             Shrewsbury.
```

Verso of Main Entry Card

tury. The "privilege" was of course much more than a courteous gesture; it was a statement backed by a royal signature which gave the author or publisher permission to print a very important kind of document—a map. The privilege mentions only the royal personage who placed his stamp of approval on the project, but it is sometimes important enough to mention in a note. Another use of the "privilege" appears in a few instances where a cartographer loaned or sold a manuscript or engraved plate to another for publication in an atlas.

(6) *Insets.*

In the analysis of the contents of a map, insets are one of the most important features to be noted. An inset is a map, chart, plan, illustration or diagram superimposed on, and usually supplementary to, a map or chart. Insets vary widely in size and importance, but they are always important enough to be noted on the catalogue card, if only as one more possible point of identification of the map proper. Any additional cataloguing, such as the making of added entry cards for each inset, should be regulated by the importance of the information contained on the inset. An inset of the city of Quebec on a general map of the St. Lawrence River is important enough to merit at least one added entry card. All insets supplying information that is supplementary to the information on the map proper should be entered on separate cards, as well as being noted on the main entry card of the map proper.

Insets are usually relegated to the corners of the map proper, but in some cases they occupy a central position, and in a few rare instances an inset is larger and more conspicuous than the main map. When there is any doubt as to which is the map and which the inset, the title of the sheet will usually help to determine the relative status of each; the title assigned to the map proper will generally be set in larger type and will occupy a more important position than the title of the inset. When a map has a very large inset, one that is equal in size and importance to the main map, or one which is larger than the map proper, both map and inset should be catalogued as though they were separate maps with cross references to each on the main entry cards.

When an inset is mentioned in a contents note, do not try to give more than a short title reference to it. Use the title given on the inset when it is clearly descriptive of the region shown, but supply a key to the region if the title of the inset is vague and uninformative. For example, "A plan of the city of Quebec . . ." is a title which will tell the reader what he wants to know about the contents of the inset. But a title such as "A view of the place where the English defeated the French in 1763 . . ." should be elucidated for the readers who will use the card catalogue. If the inset does not have a title, supply one which is brief yet descriptive of the geographical region portrayed.

Analytical cards should be made for all important insets. The cartographer of the inset will usually be the author of the map proper, but occasionally an inset was separately engraved by another cartographer and superimposed on a larger map. Then again an inset may be a reduced copy of another cartographer's work, bearing proper acknowledgments to the original author. Unless a second cartographer is mentioned in connection with the inset, the cataloguer has a right to assume that the map and the inset were made by the same individual. The imprint of the inset may also be considered the same as the imprint of the map proper unless otherwise stated. But when making analytical entries for insets which do not have the cartographer's name and the imprint repeated on them, the cataloguer should bracket on the cards all information that is taken from the map, or from any other source.

Insets are sometimes irregular in shape, and consequently difficult to measure with any degree of accuracy. When stating the dimensions of an inset which has irregular borders, give the approximate size and note the fact that it is only approximate. A note should be included in the collation line of the analytical entry stating the map is an "Inset *on* . . ." another map.

. Surprising bits of historical information are found as insets on old maps. One of the best early engravings of Independence Hall in Philadelphia is used as an inset on an eighteenth-century map of Philadelphia, published by William Faden in London. One of the earliest diagrams of a canal, showing a section of the locks used for raising and lowering boats, is found as an inset on an eighteenth-century map of the roads and inland navigation of Pennsylvania. A map of the United States by Abraham Bradley, printed in 1798, has as an inset the "Progress of the Mail on the Main Line," which is one of the earliest postal schedules established in North America, indicating the stops made by the post riders, and the time schedule between each town. This type of information is important to historical investigators, yet it is "lost" if a card is not made which will bring it to the attention of the searcher.

THE SHEET CATALOGUE

The various data listed above, all of which may be considered vital to the cataloguer and reader, cannot

MAP ACCOMPANYING A TEXT

Sotzmann, Daniel Friedrich, 1754-1840.
    Karte des nördlichsten America, nach
der zweiten ausgabe von Arrowsmith's
grosser Mercators-karte in acht blatt
gezeichnet von D. F. Sotzmann 1791.
Berlin, gestochen von Carl Jäck, 1791.
    15 7/8 x 18 1/2 in. (In Long, J.:
Reisen eines Amerikanischen Dolmetschers
und Pelzhändlers... Berlin, 1792, front.)
    No scale indicated.

Main Entry Card

        1. North America
        I. Arrowsmith, Aaron
       II. Long, John
      III. Jäck, Carl

Verso of Main Entry Card

always be crowded onto one card; this is especially true if the map title runs to any length. Rather than make one or more extension cards containing abridged or outlined information, it is better to make a sheet catalogue, which can be expanded indefinitely and which need not follow so closely the outline form selected for the card catalogue. In fact the sheet catalogue, which need be only a plain sheet of paper filed with the map itself, should be considered the place to set down bits of additional information about the map as they are acquired, or an extension or amplification of the catalogue "Notes." A few examples will illustrate the type of information which may be gathered concerning an old map.

EXAMPLE 1.

A plan of the ground allotted by His Excelance Governor Grant for the troops. No. 1. 2. 3 with a proposed plan of barracks for 720 men upon N? 2 it being the most convenient spot. n.p. [1768]

49 × 24 1/2 in. manuscript map from Gage collection.

No scale indicated.

Transmitted in Major Thomas Whitmore to Gage, St. Augustine, 10 Aug., 1768. Whitmore has consulted with Grant on the best location for the barracks. The second spot is a good situation about a mile from the town. Should it be necessary to erect barracks for officers, the first spot would be excellent. (See also Gage to Hillsborough, 7 Jan., 1769.) The engineer has placed his plan of the barracks with the kitchen, wells, etc., on the second spot.

EXAMPLE 2.

[Sowers, Thomas]

Plan of ye entrance of Pensacola harbour shewing

ye situation of the new batteries laid out & begun building in March (1771). n.p. [1771]

17 5/8 × 24 3/8 in. manuscript, tinted.

"Scale of Yards" [440 to an inch]

Shown are (1) the batteries on the "Red Cliffs" with the new powder magazine and blockhouses, (2) the new battery laid out in March, 1771 and the powder magazine on Tarter Point, (3) the new battery on the NE part of Rose Island erected in March, 1771 "which should be Stockaded as Represented in order to Secure the Old Spanish Powder Magazine." Also shown is the new blockhouse and powder magazine on the NW tip of Rose Island. MS note at upper left, "Case C. No. 27," not in Sowers' hand.

EXAMPLE 3.

Planisphere terrestre ou sont marquees [le]s longitudes de divers lieux de la terre, trouvees par les observations des eclipses des satellites de Iupiter. Dressé et presenté a sa majesté par Mr de Cassini . . . Paris, chez Iean Baptiste Nolin, 1696.

21 5/8 in. (diam.). North polar projection of the world, tinted.

No scale indicated.

The two other known copies of the Nolin imprint are in (1) Arch. Aff. Etrangères, (2) Bibliothèque Nationale. WLCL copy found laid in atlas in Vignaud collection.

A reëngraving of the original plate appears in Frederick de Wit's *Atlas maior* . . . Amsterdam [1706?] under the title *Nieuw aerdsch pleyn*, "Cornelis Danckerts Exc." No mention is made of Cassini. WLCL has second copy of the Danckerts engraving as separate. Another engraving after Cassini appears in Pieter van der Aa's *Le nouveau theatre*

ANALYTICAL CARDS FOR A MAP IN AN ATLAS

A chart of the banks of Newfoundland,
drawn from... hydrographical surveys...
of Chabert, Cook and Fleurieu... London,
Sayer & Bennett, 1775.
　　19 1/2 x 26 1/4 in. (In The North
American pilot... London, 1778-79, vol.
I, no.2)
　　Scale: 10 "Nautic Leagues" to an inch.
　　"Astronomical Observations on which
This Chart is Grounded." [table at lower
right]

Main Entry Card

　　　1. Newfoundland, Banks of
　　　I. Chabert, Joseph Bernard
　　II. Cook, James
　III. Fleurieu, Charles Pierre

Verso of Main Entry Card

```
    Newfoundland, Banks of.
    A chart of the banks of Newfoundland,
drawn from... hydrographical surveys...
of Chabert, Cook and Fleurieu... London,
Sayer & Bennett, 1775.
    19 1/2 x 26 1/4 in.  (In The North
American pilot... London, 1778-79, vol.
I, no.2)
    Scale: 10 "Nautic Leagues" to an inch.
    "Astronomical Observations on which
This Chart is Grounded." [table at lower
right]
```

First Subject Card

```
    Chabert, Joseph Bernard, Marquis de.
    A chart of the banks of Newfoundland,
drawn from... hydrographical surveys...
of Chabert, Cook and Fleurieu... London,
Sayer & Bennett, 1775.
    19 1/2 x 26 1/4 in.  (In The North
American pilot... London, 1778-79, vol.
I, no.2)
    Scale: 10 "Nautic Leagues" to an inch.
    "Astronomical Observations on which
This Chart if Grounded." [table at lower
right]
```

Added Entry Card

du monde . . . Leyden, 1713. No. 1 with French and Latin titles: *Planisphere terrestre . . . par Mr. Cassini le fils.* . . . This engraving is reproduced by Christian Sandler in *Die reformation der kartographie um 1700* . . . (Tafel II) with explanatory text [q.v.]. See also Karpinski's *Bibliography of the printed maps of Michigan* . . . Lansing, 1931, p. 39–40, 113, 117, for reproduction of WLCL original Cassini and text attributing the map to Giovanni Domenico Cassini, 1625–1712. See also Jacques Cassini's *Traité de la grandeur de la figure de la terre.* Amsterdam, 1723, for further information concerning the Observatoire Royal and the Cassinis.

TITLE CARDS

When time and space permit, it is well to make title cards for all maps, but whether or not this practice is followed, they should be made whenever there is any question of authorship. Title cards are often of great value, in that they bring reprintings and new editions together in the catalogue. Frequently the titles on old maps were only slightly altered with the printing of a new edition, and title cards appearing close together in the catalogue suggest a possible similarity in the maps themselves which inspection will sometimes verify. Anonymous maps should always be entered under the title as well as the classification heading.

SUBJECTS

Subject headings for old maps fall into two general classes: geographical and historical. Both are important. The first subject card will generally follow the classification heading assigned to the map, except in cases where the area set forth in the title does not agree with the geographical or political area selected for a classification unit in the map file (see Classifica-

78

tion). Subject headings for each map will of course vary with the collection, where it is located, who will use it, and for what purposes. The cataloguer should allow some latitude in each case and try to anticipate all possible approaches to the information available on each map.

Significant historical data should be brought out on subject cards. Important boundary lines, the tracks of explorers, the location of forts and Indian tribes, are important data to the historical investigator. A surprising number of battle plans are found superimposed on general maps. Such plans are frequently consulted and might therefore be grouped together in the catalogue under the general subject heading "Battles." Experience alone will indicate what special data should be brought out on subject cards.

CATALOGUING GEOGRAPHICAL ATLASES

Before discussing the problems related to the cataloguing of atlases, let us consider certain phases in the development of that form of book which may help to avoid possible confusion on the part of the cataloguer. The geographic atlas is probably the most unorthodox type of publication known to the book world. The format is irregular and the contents unusual. But old atlases are among the most interesting literary compilations when they are understood.

About the year 1569 or 1570 one Aegidius Hooftman, experienced mariner and patron of literature and the arts, complained to an acquaintance named Radermacher about the annoyance and inconvenience of rolling and unrolling large, cumbersome maps for study. Couldn't something be done about it? Radermacher suggested gathering all available sheet maps and binding them together in the form of a book.

Hooftman liked the suggestion. Radermacher then called upon his friend Abraham Ortel (Ortelius), map dealer and map colorer, and commissioned him to assemble all the different sheet maps available in Holland, as well as those current in France and Italy. The result was the publication in 1570 of a book of 53 maps bearing the title *Theatrum Orbis Terrarum* (The Theatre of the Whole World). The book was so popular that a second edition was published the same year. It marked the opening of a new publishing field. The mythical symbol of Atlas supporting the pillars of the sky, which were supposed to rest in the sea beyond the Western horizon, was suggested by Gerard Kremer or Krämer (Mercator), a colleague in the map publishing business. So it was that "Atlas" became a generic title as well as symbol of a collection of maps. Other titles were tried by rival map publishers, such as *Cosmographia, Theatrum* and *Speculum,* but *Atlas* was the most popular, and was retained after all others were dropped.

When cataloguing atlases as printed books, remember that from their inception, atlases were *factise,* that is, they were made up of maps acquired from many different sources and published in many different places. The atlas format, as we have seen, originated primarily as a convenient way of keeping maps together and flat. The title page, table of contents and binding were incidental and were often the only contributions made by the compiler or publisher of the volume.

Just what constitutes a perfect copy of an atlas is sometimes impossible to determine. When cataloguing an atlas as a book, take the information for the body of the card from the title page, but do not expect too much from the table of contents, if there is one. And do not call an atlas imperfect merely because copy two has ten more maps than copy one. Collate the copy you have, setting down the number of maps in *that* copy, without reference to other copies, unless you want to state in a note that the table of contents calls for so many more maps than are present, or that the copy in the Library of Congress has three more maps than your copy. Do not label your copy a cripple on the basis of the number of maps it contains.

Let us suppose a Dutch map publisher is making up fifty copies of an atlas for publication under a certain date. He has ordered and received fifty copies of a map of France from a colleague working in Paris, one of which is bound in each copy of the atlas. The map publisher sells the full edition shortly after publication, and finds he can sell twenty copies more. He has enough maps of each country to go around, except the map of France. He finds he cannot get the needed copies from Paris, so rather than disappoint his customers and change his title page, which refers to fifty maps, he inserts in place of the map of France one of Africa which he has in stock, without mentioning the change in the table of contents. This practice was quite common in the years prior to 1800, and it accounts for many of the irregularities of content found in collating two copies of the same atlas. Both copies may be just as they were the day they were published, and therefore correct for those particular copies and no others.

An atlas is only as important as the maps it contains. The information on the title page or on the main entry card may indicate in a general way what the reader can expect to find in the book, and it may tell him the number of maps it contains, but only a complete analysis of each map, treated as a separate title, will make available all the information contained in the volume. Analytical entries should follow the outline suggested for the treatment of separate maps.

All rebound atlases should be suspected of containing maps which are not included in the table of contents. Dealers and private collectors are known to bind up extra maps with atlases which have a printed table of contents calling for a smaller number of maps. All atlases should therefore be collated carefully. Maps not listed in the table of contents sometimes prove to be of greater value than those designed specifically for the atlas; in fact many rare maps have been discovered bound or laid in atlases where they do not belong. Therefore, make at least two analytical cards for every map in the atlas—a main entry card and a subject card.

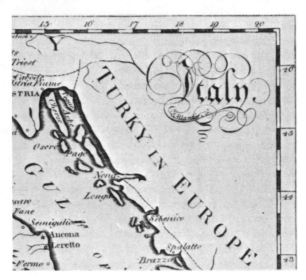

IV.

CARTOGRAPHIC NOMENCLATURE

The librarian or curator who is placed in charge of
a collection of old maps will inevitably be called upon
to answer the questions of the map collector, and
should therefore have at his command some information of a bibliographic nature to offer this type of
reader.

An old map is both a geographic tool and a bibliographic monstrosity, which involves application of the
techniques of printing and publishing, as well as etch-
ing, engraving, and other forms of graphic art. To the
collector there is magic in the words "first edition,"
and he is often more interested in priority claims than
he is in the information to be found on his maps. As
a result, it is well for the librarian to be familiar with
the terms *impression, state, issue, imprint* and *edition*,
and better still, to be able to define for the collector
the meaning of these commonly used terms. Armed
with a few good definitions and a thorough under-
standing of what they mean, the librarian can be of
great service to the collector who is not sure of what
he has bought or what he proposes to buy.

The confusion of terms used in describing old
maps rises from the fact that the processes employed
in their production are those employed in the manufacture of the kind of print usually associated with

works of art; for example, etchings, line engravings, and mezzotints, which depict scenic views, portraits and various types of still life. The natural result of this similarity of form and technique is that dealers, collectors and librarians have automatically applied the nomenclature of graphic art to old maps. And yet there have been other dealers, collectors and librarians who saw first in old maps the characteristics of printed books, pamphlets, broadsides and newspapers. It was natural for the latter group to apply to maps the nomenclature of printing, considering them first of all as publications. These two schools of thought are responsible for a steady growth of confusion in the terms employed to record descriptive data relating to maps, though both groups would probably have agreed with each other if they had been able to exchange ideas at firsthand, demonstrating concretely what feature they were describing when a given term was used. As the situation stands today, few authorities agree on the proper nomenclature to be applied to early maps. Nevertheless, if such maps are subjected to all the tests applied to the bibliography of graphic art, and all the tests employed in the bibliography of publications, per se, there is actually no conflict in the terminology commonly applied to each. Old maps must be considered from both angles if they are to be thoroughly understood and fairly appraised.

IMPRESSIONS

Having in mind the physical act involved, one may define an *impression* as the end result of pressing a sheet of paper against a plate which has on it scratches filled with ink. This impression is sometimes referred to as a *proof*. *Impression* should be thought of only as the actual transfer of markings on a plate to a sheet of paper. It is obvious, then, that the term *impression* can refer to only one specimen, as only one proof or one impression can be made at a time. Likewise, two copies of a print or map cannot be referred to as the *same impression* any more than two copies may be described as the *same proof.* But they may be called *similar impressions,* or the second copy may be called *another impression.*

STATES

The word *state,* used in reference to various forms of graphic art, has two commonly accepted meanings. The first is used to describe the physical *condition,* the relative degree of fineness, of a particular proof specimen under observation, i.e., its margins, the brilliance of the impression, the amount of foxing or staining present, and the degree to which the copy is mutilated. The second use of the word refers to the plate itself, rather than to the proof. The condition or degree of completion of the plate when copies or proofs were struck off, or "pulled," is spoken of as "the state of the plate." If, on comparing two copies of a map, it is noted that a single line has been added to, or deleted from, the plate before the second copy was made, the maps are said to represent different *states of the plate,* and the two proofs under observation are said to be different *states of the map.*

Used in the first sense, *state* may include such fine points of printing as the weight and make of the paper used in pulling proofs or making impressions. It may also refer to watermarks in the paper, and the amount of ink or color used to get the resulting effect. The map is said to be in "fine state" or "fine condition." It is a "fine copy." But in the second sense, the state of a map changes only when a change of any sort, however small, is made in the plate itself. It is with this second sense of the word *state* that we are concerned.

Although this second use of the word is not uncommon, its exact meaning is not always clear, because dealers, collectors, librarians and bibliographers insist on numbering states consecutively before all the evidence is in. It does not necessarily follow that because a map represents a later state of the plate than a first copy it must always be the *second* state. Impressions may have been taken from the plate at several intermediate stages which are not available for comparison. And too, it is not always easy to determine by a careful comparison of two copies of a map, representing two states of a plate, which is earlier. Usually the copy which has been corrected, or added to, is the later state, but not always. These complications are mentioned because bibliographies and catalogues are sometimes cluttered with such statements as "a second variant of the third state," or "an intermediate state," all of which means very little except that differences have been noted, or other copies discovered, which were not known when the numbering began.

Unless there is concrete proof available to support the claim, it is wise to refer to "another state" instead of "the second state." It is most inconvenient to find, after numbering a first and second state of a map, that there is another state which comes between the first state and what you thought was the second. Leave an opening for future discoveries; the last word has not been said in any field of investigation.

ISSUES OR PRINTINGS

The word *issue* is usually associated with the printing or publication of a work: the routine of production. Here there is an overlapping of terms, as the two preceding definitions concern the map only as a specimen of engraving. *Issues* and *editions* are terms which derive from the nomenclature of book publishing, and which concern the map as an end product of printing *and nothing else.*

In the printing of books, an issue refers to the number of copies or impressions struck off from the plates *at a given time.* For the sake of clarity the term can be narrowed, and frequently is, when used in connection with old maps and prints, to mean the number of impressions (copies) made at a given time *without any change being made in the plate.* This narrower definition would also apply to the printing of books, in almost every case, but there are enough exceptions to the rule to make it advisable to be more specific when applying the term to maps and prints. But inasmuch as the term *issue* is applied, almost universally, to *the number of copies made at a given time,* it seems logical to go a step further in the case of maps and include the phrase "without alteration of the plate."

In order to determine the existence of different issues of a map, it is necessary to study the internal evidence on the map itself, noting changes in the *state of the plate* made by the engraver. There is no way of knowing how many copies were pulled from a plate at a given time unless the printer left some record, which is seldom the case. The word *issue,* then, is a relative term used to differentiate between copies of the same map printed at different times, characterized by changes made in the plate between the two printings. An issue represents, too, all the *copies* which were printed before a change was made in the plate. The presence of two *states* of a map implies automatically that there were two *issues* of that map printed.

87

EDITIONS

An *edition*, in the case of old maps, is determined by one thing only—*the imprint:* namely, the place of publication, the printer and/or the publisher and date. An edition may be defined, then, as the number of copies of a map which were printed by the same man, or men, at a given place and under a given publication date. Some old maps do not bear a complete imprint, but usually there is a place of publication and the name of the printer or publisher is given. Of the three pieces of information comprising the imprint, the date is most frequently omitted. This fact is not hard to understand when maps are found which were published and republished over a period of forty years. It was easier to leave out the date altogether than it was to remove the first and engrave another every time the map was republished.

If any change occurs in any part of the imprint, it is safe to say there was a change in the "editing" or publishing. The plate from which the map was made may have been sold to another publisher, transported to another city or reissued at another time. But whether or not the date has been altered, a change of place or a change of publisher implies a new edition. This is true even though two copies are identical in every respect except the imprint. When a map bears no imprint, it must be described in generalities: it is an *impression,* because it is a printed map. It is one specimen of an *issue* or *printing* made at a given time. The complete issue, of *x* number of copies, was, because there is no imprint on the map, printed anonymously on an unrecorded date.

Caution is recommended when speaking about the different editions of a map. Even when two copies of a map are dated only a year apart, it does not necessarily follow that the second copy is a *second* edition. It may well be the third or fourth edition. Likewise, there are cases on record where a map was republished more than once in the same year, with perhaps a change in the place of publication or else a change of printer or publisher. Label a map "first edition" only when it is so stated on the map itself, or when the information is clearly stated somewhere else, as in a contemporary newspaper announcement, or in the records of Stationers' Hall or in some other official, reliable source. If this procedure is followed, there should be no confusion of terms in connection with map publication.

In conclusion, it may be said that a change in the *state* of the plate, including any printed matter that is part of the plate, such as a description or legend, implies a new *issue*. A "variant" copy of a map, with the same imprint, is the same as "another issue." It is a "variant issue" or a "different issue." A change in the *state* of the *imprint,* whether the map has any other changes on it or not, implies "a new edition," a "different edition." The state of the plate can be changed any number of times by changing the markings on the plate. Any number of issues may be included in the same edition. Regardless of the changes which occur on the rest of the plate, a new *edition* is produced only when some change is made in the imprint: either in the place of publication, the printer and/or the publisher or the date. According to the above definitions, the terms *impression, state, issue* and *edition* are not interchangeable, and there should be no confusion concerning them.

LIST OF REFERENCES

GENERAL

AMERICAN LIBRARY ASSOCIATION. *Catalog rules: author and title entries.* Comp. by committees of the American library association and the (British) library association. American ed. Boston, A. L. A. publishing board, 1908. [preliminary revised edition in process]

BOGGS, S. W., and LEWIS, DOROTHY C. *Classification and cataloging of maps and atlases.* (Mimeographed.) Washington, 1932.

BRIQUET, CHARLES MOÏSE. *Les filigranes;* dictionnaire historique des marques du papier dès leur apparition vers 1282 jusqu'en 1600 . . . Leipzig, Hiersemann, 1923.

BRUNET, JACQUES CHARLES. *Manuel du libraire et de l'amateur de livres* . . . Paris, Firmin Didot, 1860–65.

CUTTER, CHARLES A. *Rules for a dictionary catalog.* 4th ed. Washington, Govt. print. off., 1904.

A DICTIONARY *of the printers and booksellers who were at work in England, Scotland, and Ireland from 1726 to 1775:* those in England by H. R. Plomer, Scotland by G. H. Bushnell, Ireland by E. R. McC. Dix. [Oxford] Printed for the Bibliographical society at the Oxford univ. pr., 1932.

ECKERT, MAX. *Die kartenwissenschaft forsuchungen und grundlagen zu einer kartographie als wissenschaft.* Berlin und Leipzig, W. de Gruyter, 1921–25.

HEAWOOD, EDWARD. *The use of watermarks in dating old maps and documents* . . . London, Royal geographical society, 1924.

HOLDEN, JOHN ALLAN. *The bookman's glossary;* a compendium of information relating to the production and distribution of books. 2d ed., rev. and enl. New York, R. R. Bowker; London, D. H. Bond, 1931.

HUNTER, DARD. *Papermaking through eighteen centuries* . . . New York, W. E. Rudge, 1930.

KNOX, ALEXANDER. *Glossary of geographical and topographical terms* and of words of frequent occurrence in the composition of such terms and of place-names. London, E. Stanford, 1904.

LAUSSEDAT, AIMÉ. *Histoire de la cartographie;* conférence faite à l'Ecole des hautes études commerciales, sous le patronage de la Société centrale du travail professionnel. Paris, Administration des deux revues, 1892.

LELEWEL, JOACHIM. *Géographie du moyen âge;* étudiée, accompagné d'atlas et de cartes dans chaque volume . . . Bruxelles, V^e et J. Pilliet, 1850–52.

—— *Epilogue de la Géographie du moyen âge;* étudiée accompagné de huit planches. Bruxelles, V^e et J. Pilliet, 1857.

LEYSER, POLYCARPUS. *Polycarpi Leyser* . . . *commentatio de vera geographiae methodo;* inseritvr specimen atlantis et selecti et ivsto ordine digesti. Helmstadii, typis Pavli Dieterici Schnorrii, 1726.

MANN, MARGARET. *Introduction to cataloging and the classification of books.* Chicago, A. L. A., 1930. [revised ed. in process]

MINNESOTA HISTORICAL SOCIETY. *Copying manuscripts;* rules worked out by the Minnesota historical society, Manuscript division, Grace Lee Nute, curator. (Half-title: Publications of the Minnesota historical society . . . Special bulletins, II.) Saint Paul, Minnesota historical society, 1935.

NORDENSKIÖLD, NILS ADOLF ERIK, friherre. *Periplus; an essay on the early history of charts and sailing-directions;* tr. from the Swedish original by Francis A. Bather. Stockholm, [P. A. Norstedt & soner] 1897.

SALISBURY, ROLLIN D., and ATWOOD, WALLACE W. *The interpretation of topographic maps.* (U. S. Geological survey, Professional paper 60.) Washington, Govt. print. off., 1908.

SANDLER, CHRISTIAN. *Die reformation der kartographie um 1700;* mit 4 tabellarischen und text-beilagen und 6 kartentafeln. München und Berlin, R. Oldenbourg, 1905.

STEIN, HENRI. *Manuel de bibliographie générale.* (Bibliotheca bibliographica nova.) Paris, A. Picard et fils, 1897.

STILLWELL, MARGARET BINGHAM. *Incunabula and Americana,* 1450–1800; a key to bibliographical study . . . New York, Columbia univ. pr., 1931.

U. S. LIBRARY OF CONGRESS. DIVISION OF BIBLIOGRAPHY. *List of books (with references to periodicals) relating to the theory of colonization, government of dependencies, protectorates, and related topics,* by

93

A. P. C. Griffin . . . 2d ed., with additions. Washington, Govt. print. off., 1900.

—— —— DIVISION OF MAPS. *Noteworthy maps . . . no.* [1]–3 Accessions . . . with acknowledgement of sources of gifts, exchanges, and transfers. 1925/26–1927/28. Washington, Govt. print. off., 1927–30.

WINSOR, JUSTIN, ed. *Narrative and critical history of America,* by a corps of eminent historical scholars and specialists . . . Standard library ed. [Boston, Houghton Mifflin & Co., 1923, c1884–89]

CARE AND REPAIR

KOHL, JOHANN GEORG. *Substance of a lecture delivered at the Smithsonian institution on a collection of the charts and maps of America.* (In Smithsonian institution. Annual report, 1856. Washington, 1857, p. 93–146.)

LYDENBERG, HARRY MILLER, and ARCHER, JOHN. *The care and repair of books.* New York, Bowker, 1931.

ST. LOUIS, PUBLIC LIBRARY. *Maps in the St. Louis public library,* by Mildred Boatman . . . [St. Louis, the Library] 1931.

U. S. LIBRARY OF CONGRESS. DIVISION OF MANUSCRIPTS. *Notes on the care, cataloguing, calendaring and arranging of manuscripts;* 2d ed., by J. C. Fitzpatrick. Washington, Govt. print. off., 1921.

MAP MAKING

ADAMS, CYRUS CORNELIUS. *"Maps and map-making,"* *Amer. Geog. Soc. Bull.,* 44 (1912), 194–201.

BLAKIE, W. B. *How maps are made.* (In Smithsonian institution. Annual report, 1893. Washington, 1894, p. 419–433, pl. XXI–XXII.)

ECKERT, MAX. *"On the nature of maps and map logic";* tr. by W. Joerg, *Amer. Geog. Soc. Bull.,* 40 (1908), 344–51.

FORDHAM, SIR HERBERT GEORGE. *Note sur la liaison entre la cartobibliographie et l'histoire.* Bruxelles, Imp. P. Dykmans (succ. de A. Berqueman), 1923.

GALLOIS, LUCIEN LOUIS JOSEPH. *Les géographes allemands de la renaissance . . .* (Bibliothèque de la Faculté des lettres de Lyon. Tome XIII.) Paris, E. Leroux, 1890.

HINKS, ARTHUR ROBERT. *Maps and survey.* Cambridge, Univ. pr., 1913.

HOLMAN, LOUIS ARTHUR. *Old maps and their makers* considered from the historical & decorative standpoints; a survey of a huge subject in a small space. Boston, C. E. Goodspeed, 1925.

HUMPHREYS, ARTHUR LEE. *Old decorative maps and charts;* with illustrations from engravings in the Macpherson collection, and a catalogue of the atlases, etc., in the collection, by Henry Stevens. London, Halton & T. Smith, ltd.; New York, Minton, Balch & Co., 1926.

MORRISON, GABRIEL JAMES. *Maps, their uses and construction;* a short popular treatise on the advantages and defects of maps on various projections, followed by an outline of the principles involved in their construction . . . 2d ed., rev. and enl. London, E. Stanford, 1902.

REEVES, EDWARD AYEARST. *The mapping of the earth, past, present, and future.* [London, William Clowes and sons, ltd.] 1916; Reprinted from the *Geographical Journal,* October, 1916.

—— *Maps and map-making;* three lectures delivered under the auspices of the Royal geographical society . . . London, Royal geographical society, 1910.

SLAFTER, EDMUND FARWELL. *History and causes of the incorrect latitudes as recorded in the journals of the early writers, navigators and explorers relating to the Atlantic coast of North America, 1535–1740.* Boston, Priv. print. [D. Clapp and son, printers] 1882; Reprinted from the *New England Historical and Genealogical Register,* April, 1882.

THIELE, WALTER. *Official map publications;* a historical sketch, and a bibliographical handbook of current maps and mapping services in the United States, Canada, Latin America, France, Great Britain, Germany, and certain other countries . . . under the direction of A. F. Kuhlman. (Planographed.) Chicago, A. L. A., 1938.

U. S. COAST AND GEODETIC SURVEY. *Elements of map projection* with applications to map and chart construction, by Charles H. Deetz and Oscar S. Adams . . . (Special publication, no. 68.) Washington, Govt. print. off., 1931.

WINSLOW, ARTHUR. *The mapping of Missouri.* Academy of science of St. Louis, *Transactions,* VI, no. 3 (1892).

WINTERBOTHAM, HAROLD ST. JOHN LOYD. *A key to maps* . . . [Blackie's "Key" series] London, Blackie, [1936]

WRIGHT, JOHN KIRTLAND. *Early topographical maps,*
their geographical and historical value as illustrated
by maps of the Harrison collection of the American
geographical society . . . (Library series, no. 3.)
New York, American geographical society, 1924.

HISTORICAL SKETCHES

BRITISH MUSEUM. DEPARTMENT OF PRINTS & DRAWINGS.
A guide to the processes and schools of engraving;
with notes on some of the most important masters
[by Arthur M. Hind] 2d ed. [London] Printed by
order of the trustees of the British museum, 1923.

DAHLGREN, ERIK WILHELM. *Les débuts de la cartographie du Japon.* (Archives d'études orientales; publiées par J. A. Lundell, v.4.) Upsal [K. W. Appel-
bergs boktryckeri] 1911.

FISCHER, THEOBALD, ed. *Sammlung mittelalterlicher
welt- und seekarten italienischen ursprungs und
aus italienischen bibliotheken und archiven . . .*
(Beiträge zur geschichte der erdkunde und der
kartographie in Italien im mittelalter.) Venedig, F.
Ongania, 1886.

FORDHAM, SIR HERBERT GEORGE. *Studies in carto-
bibliography, British and French,* and in the bibliography of itineraries and road-books. Oxford,
Clarendon pr., 1914.

A GENERAL COLLECTION *of voyages:* undertaken either
for discovery, conquest, settlement, or the opening
of trade, from the commencement of the Portuguese discoveries, to the present time. Vol. I. London, Pub. by W. Richardson [1789]

HAMY, JULES THÉODORE ERNEST. *Portolan charts of the* xv*th,* xvi*th, & * xvii*th centuries* collected by the late Dr. Theodore. Hamy. [New York, 1912]

KOHL, JOHANN GEORG. *Asia and America;* an historical disquisition concerning the ideas which former geographers had about the geographical relation and connection of the Old and New world. [Worcester, Mass., U. S. A., The Society, 1911]; Reprinted from the Proceedings of the American antiquarian society, October, 1911.

—— *Substance of a lecture delivered at the Smithsonian institution on a collection of the charts and maps of America.* (In Smithsonian institution. Annual report, 1856. Washington, 1857, p. 93–146.)

SCAIFE, WALTER BELL. *America: its geographical history,* 1492–1892; six lectures delivered to graduate students of the Johns Hopkins university; with a supplement entitled Was the Rio del Espiritu Santo of the Spanish geographers the Mississippi? Baltimore, Johns Hopkins pr., 1892.

STEVENSON, EDWARD LUTHER. *Portolan charts;* their origin and characteristics, with a descriptive list of those belonging to the Hispanic society of America. New York [Knickerbocker pr.] 1911.

—— *Terrestrial and celestial globes;* their history and construction, including a consideration of their value as aids in the study of geography and astronomy . . . New Haven, Pub. for the Hispanic society of America by the Yale univ. pr., 1921.

THACHER, JOHN BOYD. *The continent of America:* its discovery and its baptism; an essay on the nomenclature of the old continents; a critical and bibliographical inquiry into the naming of America and into the growth of the cosmography of the New world; together with an attempt to establish the landfall of Columbus on Watling Island, and the subsequent discoveries and explorations on the main land by Americus Vespucius. New York, W. E. Benjamin, 1896.

TIELE, PIETER ANTON, ed. *Mémoire bibliographique sur les journaux des navigateurs néerlandais* réimprimés dans les collections de de Bry et de Hulsius, et dans les collections hollandaises du XVII siècle, et sur les anciennes éditions hollandaises des journaux de navigateurs étrangers; la plupart en la possession de Frederik Muller; avec tables des voyages, des éditions et des matières. Amsterdam, F. Muller, 1867.

UZIELLI, GUSTAVO, and AMAT DI S. FILIPPO, P. *Mappamondi, carte nautiche, portolani ed altri monumenti cartografici specialmente italiani dei secoli* XIII–XVII. Ed. 2. Roma, Società [geografica italiana] 1882.

WALCKENAER, CHARLES ATHANESE, baron. *Recherches sur la géographie ancienne* et sur celle du moyen âge . . . A Paris, de l'Imprimerie royale, 1823; Extrait des tomes V, VI et VII des Mémoires de l'Académie des inscriptions et belles-lettres.

BIOBIBLIOGRAPHIES

BAGROW, LEO, ed. *A. Ortellii catalogus cartographorum.* (Ergänzungsheft nr. 199 & 210 zu "Petermanns mitteilungen.") Gotha, J. Perthes, 1928–30.

BAUDET, PIERRE JOSEPH HENRY. *Leven en werken van Willem Jansz. Blaeu;* uitg. door het Provinciaal

Utrechtsch genootschap van kunsten en wetenschappen. Utrecht, C. van der Post, jr., 1871.

—— Notice sur la part prise par Willem Jansz. Blaeu (1571–1638) dans la détermination des longitudes terrestres. Utrecht, K. A. Manssen [1875]

HALL, ELIAL F. *Gerard Mercator: his life and works* . . . (Bulletin, no. 4, 1878.) New York, Printed for the [American geographical] society, 1878.

HARRISSE, HENRY. *La cartographie Verrazaniene* . . . Paris, Institut géographique de Paris; C. Delagrave, 1896; Extrait de la Revue de géographie.

JOMARD, EDME FRANCOIS. *Introduction à l'atlas des monuments de la géographie* . . . publiée par les soins et avec des remarques de M. E. Cortambert . . . Paris, A. Bertrand, 1879; Extrait du Bulletin de la Société de géographie de Paris.

NOTICE *des Ouvrages de m. D'Anville,* premier géographe du roi, membre de l'Académie des inscriptions et belles-lettres, et de l'Académie des science de Paris . . . précédée de son éloge [par m. Dacier] A Paris, Chez Fuchs, Demanne, de l'Imprimerie de Delance, An X (1802).

"Catalogue des cartes gravées d'aprés les dessins de m. D'Anville," p. 45–102; "Catalogue des ouvrages imprimés de m. D'Anville," p. 103–20.

ORTROY, FERNAND GRATIEN VAN. *Bibliographie de l'oeuvre de Pierre Apian.* Besancon, Paul Jacquin, 1902; Extrait du Bibliographe moderne, mars–octobre, 1901.

—— *Bio-bibliographie de Gemma Frisius,* fondateur de l'école belge de geographie de son fils Corneille et de ses neveux les Arsenius . . . [Bruxelles, M. Hayez, 1920]; Extrait des Mémoires publiés par l'Académie royale de Belgique.

POGO, ALEXANDER. *Gemma Frisius, his method of determining differences of longitude by transporting timepieces (1530), and his treatise on triangulation (1533)* . . . Bruges, Saint Catherine pr., ltd. [1935]; Reprinted from *Isis*, XXII, 2, no. 64, (February, 1935).

RAEMDONCK, J. VAN. *Gérard Mercator; sa vie et ses oeuvres.* St. Nicholas, Chez E. Dalschaert-Praet, 1869.

STEVENSON, EDWARD LUTHER. *Early Spanish cartography of the New world,* with special reference to the Wolfenbüttel-Spanish map and the work of Diego Ribero . . . [Worcester, Mass., Davis pr., 1909]

TIELE, PIETER ANTON. *Nederlandsche bibliographie van land- en volkenkunde;* Amsterdam, F. Muller en comp., 1884.

WAUWERMANS, HENRI EMMANUEL. *Histoire de l'ecole cartographique belge et anversoise du* XVIe *siècle* . . . Bruxelles, Institut national de géographie, 1895.

REGIONAL STUDIES

BALDWIN, CHARLES CANDEE. *Early maps of Ohio and the West.* [Cleveland] Fairbanks, Benedict & co., 1875.

[BOIMARE, A. L.] *Notes bibliographiques et raisonnées sur les principaux ouvrages publiés sur la Floride et l'ancienne Louisiane,* depuis leur découverte jusqu'à l'époque actuelle; accompagnées de trois cartes, de Guillaume Delisle, publiées en 1703 et 1712. [Paris, priv. lithographed, 1855]

FITE, EMERSON DAVID, and FREEMAN, ARCHIBALD, comps. and eds. *A book of old maps,* delineating American history from the earliest days down to the close of the revolutionary war . . . Cambridge, Harvard univ. pr., 1926.

GANONG, WILLIAM FRANCIS. *The cartography of the Gulf of St. Lawrence,* from Cartier to Champlain. [Ottawa, J. Durie & son. 1889]

—— *A monograph of the cartography of the province of New Brunswick.* Ottawa, J. Durie & son, 1897.

GRIFFIN, APPLETON PRENTISS CLARK. *The discovery of the Mississippi;* a bibliographical account, with a fac-simile of the map of Louis Joliet, 1674 . . . to which is appended a note on the Joliet map, by B. F. De Costa . . . with a sketch of Joutel's maps . . . New York, A. S. Barnes, 1883.

HAMY, JULES THÉODORE ERNEST. *Les origines de la cartographie de l'Europe septentrionale* . . . Paris, E. Leroux, 1889.

[HARRISSE, HENRY] *Notes pour servir à l'histoire, à la bibliographie et à la cartographie de la Nouvelle-France et des pays adjacents 1545–1700.* Par l'auteur de la Bibliotheca americana vetustissima . . . Paris, Tross, 1872.

KARPINSKI, LOUIS CHARLES. *Historical atlas of the Great Lakes and Michigan,* to accompany the Bibliography of the printed maps of Michigan . . . Lansing, Michigan historical commission, 1931.

KOHL, JOHANN GEORG. *History of discovery and exploration on the coasts of the United States.* ([U. S. Coast and geodetic survey. Report of the superintendent, 1884] Appendix no. 19.) [Washington, Govt. print. off., 1885]

KUNSTMANN, FRIEDRICH. *Die entdeckung Amerikas;* nach den ältesten quellen geschichtlich dargestellt; mit einem atlas alter bisher ungedruckter karten. München, In commission bei A. Asher & Cⁱᵉ in Berlin, 1859.

MARCEL, GABRIEL ALEXANDRE. *Cartographie de la Nouvelle France.* Supplément à l'ouvrage de m. Harrisse; publié avec des documents inédits Gabriel Marcel . . . Paris, Maisonneuve frères et C. Leclerc, 1885; Extrait de la Revue de géographie.

PHILLIPS, PHILIP LEE. *Guiana and Venezuela cartography.* Reprinted from American historical association. Annual report . . . for the year 1897. Washington, 1898, p. 681–776.

—— *Virginia cartography;* a bibliographical description. Washington, Smithsonian institution, 1896.

PROWSE, GEORGE ROBERT FARRAR. *Exploration of the Gulf of St. Lawrence, 1499–1525.* (Mimeographed.) Winnipeg, the Author, 1929.

RUGE, SOPHUS. *The development of the cartography of America up to the year 1570.* Reprinted from Smithsonian institution. Annual report, 1894. Washington, 1896, p. 281–296, pl. XVII–XLV.

SANTAREM, MANUEL FRANCISCO DE BARROS, 2. VISCONDE DE. *Estudos de cartographia antiga* . . . [Lisboa, Typ. de Alfredo Lamas, Motta & c.ᵃ.l.ᵈᵃ., Imprensa Portugal-Brazil l.ᵈᵃ, 1919–20]

STEVENSON, EDWARD LUTHER. *Maps illustrating early discovery and exploration in America, 1502–1530.* Reproduced by photography from the original manuscripts . . . New Brunswick, N. J., 1906.

STOKES, ISAAC NEWTON PHELPS. *The iconography of Manhattan island, 1498, 1909,* compiled from original sovrces and illvstrated by photointaglio reprodvctions of important maps, plans, views and docvments in pvblic and private collections . . . New York, R. H. Dodd, 1915–28.

THOMASSY, RAYMOND, i.e. MARIE JOSEPH RAYMOND. *Cartographie de la Louisiane* . . . Paris, Librairie scientifique, industrielle et agricole ₍1860?₎

THOMPSON, EDMUND. *Maps of Connecticut before the year 1800.* Windham, Hawthorn House, 1940.

WILGUS, ALVA CURTIS, comp. *Maps relating to Latin America in books and periodicals* . . . (₍Pan American union. Columbus memorial library₎ Bibliographic series, no. 10.) Washington, Pan American union, 1933.

WINSOR, JUSTIN. *Cartier to Frontenac* . . . Geographical discovery in the interior of North America in its historical relations, 1534–1700; with full cartographical illustrations from contemporary sources . . . Boston, Houghton Mifflin & Co., 1894.

₍—— ed.₎ *"The cartography of the northeast coast of* ₍North₎ America . . . ₍1535–1600₎," . . . (In his Narrative and critical history of America. Boston, 1884–89, v. 4 (1885), p. ₍81₎–102.)

₍——₎ *"The earliest maps of the Spanish and Portuguese discoveries."* . . . (In his Narrative and critical history of America. Boston, 1884–89, v. 2 (1886), p. ₍93₎–128.)

[⸻] *"The early cartography of the Gulf of Mexico and adjacent parts."* . . . (In his Narrative and critical history of America. Boston, 1884–89, v. 2 (1886), p. [217]–230.)

CATALOGUES AND CHECK LISTS

ADAMS, RANDOLPH GREENFIELD. *British headquarters maps and sketches used by Sir Henry Clinton while in command of the British forces operating in North America during the war for independence, 1775–1782: a descriptive list of the original manuscripts and printed documents now preserved in the William L. Clements library at the University of Michigan* . . . Ann Arbor, William L. Clements library, 1928.

BOSTON. ENGINEERING DEPARTMENT. *List of maps of Boston published between 1600 and 1903,* copies of which are to be found in the possession of the city of Boston or other collectors of the same . . . Boston, Municipal print. off., 1903.

BRITISH MUSEUM. DEPARTMENT OF MANUSCRIPTS. *Catalogue of the manuscript maps, charts, and plans, and of the topographical drawings in the British museum* . . . London, Printed by order of the Trustees, 1844–61.

⸻ DEPARTMENT OF PRINTED BOOKS. KING'S LIBRARY. *Catalogue of maps, prints, drawings, etc. forming the geographical and topographical collection attached to the library of His late Majesty George the Third,* and presented by His Majesty King George the Fourth to the British museum . . . London, Printed by order of the Trustees of the British museum, by G. Woodfall, 1829.

—— —— MAP ROOM. *Cartografía cubana del British museum;* catálogo cronologico de cartas, planos y mapas de los siglos XVI al XIX. Por Domingo Figarola-Caneda . . . 2. ed., corr. Habana, Impr. de la Biblioteca nacional, 1910.

—— —— —— *Catalogue of the printed maps, plans, and charts in the British museum.* London, Printed by order of the Trustees, 1885.

CANADA. ARCHIVES. *Catalogue of maps, plans and charts in the Map room of the Dominion archives,* classified and indexed by H. R. Holmden, in charge of the Map division. Published by authority of the secretary of state under the direction of the archivist. (Publications of the Canadian archives, no. 8.) Ottawa, Govt. print. bur., 1912.

—— GEOGRAPHIC BOARD. *Catalogue of the maps in the collection of the Geographic board;* list of the maps cor. to 1st January, 1922. Ottawa, F. A. Acland, printer to the King's Most Excellent Majesty, 1922.

DIONNE, NARCISSE EUTROPE. *Inventaire chronologique* . . . Quebec [Royal Society of Canada] 1905–09.
    Contents: t.4. Inventaire chronologique des cartes, plans, atlas relatifs à la Nouvelle-France et à la province de Québec, 1508–1908.

DUBLIN UNIVERSITY. TRINITY COLLEGE. LIBRARY. *Catalogue of the manuscripts in the library* . . . to which is added a list of the Fagel collection of maps in the same library; comp. by T. K. Abbott . . . (librarian). Dublin, Hodges, Figgis, & co., ltd.; London, Longmans, Green & Co., 1900.

[EAMES, WILBERFORCE] *A list of editions of Ptolemy's geography* 1475–1730. New York, 1886; Reprinted from Sabin's *Bibliotheca Americana.*

106

FADEN, WILLIAM. *Catalogue of a curious and valuable collection of original maps and plans of military positions held in the old French and revolutionary wars;* with plans of different cities, and maps of the country . . . This collection was . . . made by an American gentleman who had access to the collection of William Faden . . . Boston [J. Wilson & son, printers] 1862.

——, and JEFFERYS, THOMAS. *Catalogue des cartes, plans, et cartes-marines, tirés des pays étrangers* . . . A Londres, Mars, 1774.

—— —— *A catalogue of modern and correct maps, plans, and charts* . . . London, Sold by Faden, and Jefferys, geographer to the king, January, 1774.

FRANCE. SERVICE HYDROGRAPHIQUE. *Catalogue des cartes, plans, instructions nautiques, mémoires, etc., qui composent l'hydrographie francaise au 1er janvier 1925.* Paris, Imprimerie nationale, 1925.

HARVARD UNIVERSITY. LIBRARY. *A catalogue of the library* . . . (Vol. 3, pt. 2 has title: A catalogue of the maps and charts in the Library of Harvard university in Cambridge, Massachusetts.) Cambridge, E. W. Metcalf and co., 1830–31.

HASKELL, DANIEL CARL. *Manhattan maps;* a co-operative list . . . New York, The New York public library, 1931.

HENRY E. HUNTINGTON LIBRARY AND ART GALLERY. *A catalogue of maps of America from the sixteenth to the nineteenth centuries.* (No. 93 of the catalogues of the Museum book store. "The items described in this catalogue now form a part of the collection of the Henry E. Huntington library and art gallery.") London, Museum book store, 1924.

KARPINSKI, LOUIS CHARLES. *Bibliography of the printed maps of Michigan*, 1804–1880, with a series of over one hundred reproductions of maps constituting an historical atlas of the Great Lakes and Michigan . . . including discussions of Michigan maps and map-makers, by William Lee Jenks . . . Lansing, Michigan historical commission, 1931.

LOBANOV-ROSTOVSKIĬ, ALEKSANDR IAKOVLEVICH, *kni͡az.* *Catalogue des cartes géographiques, topographiques, & marines* . . . suivi d'une notice de manuscrits. Paris, Firmin Didot, 1823.

LOWERY, WOODBURY. *The Lowery collection;* a descriptive list of maps of the Spanish possessions within the present limits of the United States, 1502–1820 . . . ed. with notes by Philip Lee Phillips . . . Washington, Govt. print. off., 1912.

NEW YORK. PUBLIC LIBRARY. *List of maps of the world,* illustrating the progress of geographical knowledge from the earliest time to the end of the seventeenth century. Exhibited in the Lenox branch . . . on the occasion of the visit of the members of the eighth International geographical congress. New York [New York Public Library] 1904.

—— —— ARTS AND PRINTS DIVISION. *American historical prints,* early views of American cities, etc., from the Phelps Stokes and other collections, by I. N. Phelps Stokes and D. C. Haskell . . . New York, New York public library, 1932.

NEW YORK. STATE LIBRARY. *Catalogue of New-York state library:* 1856; maps, manuscripts, engravings, coins, &c. Albany, C. Van Benthuysen, 1857.

NEWBERRY LIBRARY. *List of manuscript maps in the Edward E. Ayer collection;* comp. by Clara A. Smith. (Multigraphed.) Chicago, Newberry library, 1927.

PARIS. BIBLIOTHÈQUE NATIONALE. *Catalogue des documents géographiques exposés à la Section des cartes et plans de la Bibliothèque nationale.* Paris, J. Maisonneuve, 1892.

—— DÉPARTEMENT DES IMPRIMÉS. *Notice des documents exposés à la Section cartes,* plans et collections géographiques du Département . . . (In Revue des bibliothèques, 22 (1912), p. ₁₃₇₁–197.)

PHILLIPS, PHILIP LEE. *Alaska and the northwest part of North America,* 1588–1898: maps in the Library of Congress. Washington, Govt. print. off., 1898.

SHURTLEFF, NATHANIEL B. *List of the printed maps of Boston* . . . Boston, Municipal print. off., 1863.

SOCIETÀ ITALIANA PER IL PROGRESSO DELLE SCIENZE. 1ST CONGRESS, PARMA, 1907. *Esposizione di cartografia parmigiana e piacentina nel salone della Palatina.* Catalogo compilato dal prof. dottor Umberto Benassi. Parma, Tip. oper. Adorni-Ugolotti e c., 1907.

TORONTO. PUBLIC LIBRARY. *Map collection of the public reference library.* Toronto, Public library, 1923.

TORRES LANZAS, PEDRO. *Relacion descriptiva de los mapas, planos, &* ₁!₁, *de México y Floridas,* existentes en el Archivo general de Indias . . . Sevilla, Imp. de El Mercantil, 1900.

—— *Relacion descriptiva de los mapas, planos, etc. de la audiencia y capitanía general de Guatemala* <Guatemala, San Salvador, Honduras, Nicaragua y Costa-Rica> existentes en el Archivo general de

Indias . . . Madrid, Tip de la Revista de arch., bibl. y museos, 1903.

U. S. Board of Surveys and Maps. *Map collections in the District of Columbia;* compiled by the Committee on information, January, 1930. Rev. and reprinted July, 1932. (Lithographed.) ₍Washington, prepared by the U. S. Geological Survey₎

—— Library of Congress. Division of Maps. *A list of geographical atlases in the Library of Congress,* with bibliographical notes; comp. under the direction of Philip Lee Phillips . . . Washington, Govt. print. off., 1909–20.

—— —— —— *A list of maps of America in the Library of Congress,* preceded by a list of works relating to cartography; by P. Lee Phillips . . . Washington, Govt. print. off., 1901.

Uricoechea, Ezequiel. *Mapoteca colombiana.* Coleccion de los títulos de todos los mapas, planos, vistas etc. relativos á la América española, Brasil é islas adyacentes; arreglada cronologicamente i precedida de una introduccion sobre la historia cartográfica de América . . . Lóndres, Trübner y cía, 1860.

Winsor, Justin. *The Kohl collection of maps relating to America.* (Bibliographical contributions . . . no. 19.) Cambridge, The Library of Harvard univ., 1886.